01237283

Mary Mapes Dodge

Twayne's United States Authors Series
Children's Literature

Ruth K. MacDonald, Editor
Purdue University Calumet

TUSAS 604

Mary Mapes Dodge at the time of the founding of *St. Nicholas*. Princeton University Library. Reproduced by permission.

Mary Mapes Dodge

Susan R. Gannon
and Ruth Anne Thompson

*The Dyson College of
Pace University*

Twayne Publishers ● New York
Maxwell Macmillan Canada ● *Toronto*
Maxwell Macmillan International ● *New York Oxford Singapore Sydney*

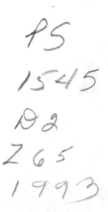

Mary Mapes Dodge
Susan R. Gannon and Ruth Anne Thompson

Twayne Publishers
Macmillan Publishing Company
866 Third Avenue
New York, New York 10022

Maxwell Macmillan Canada, Inc.
1200 Eglinton Avenue East
Suite 200
Don Mills, Ontario M3C 3N1

Macmillan Publishing Company is part of the Maxwell Communication
Group of Companies.

Library of Congress Cataloging-in-Publication Data

Gannon, Susan R.
    Mary Mapes Dodge / by Susan R. Gannon and Ruth Anne Thompson.
        p.   cm.—(Twayne United States authors series)
    Includes bibliographical references and index.
    ISBN 0-8057-3956-4
    1. Dodge, Mary Mapes, 1830–1905—Criticism and interpretation.
    I. Thompson, Ruth Anne.   II. Title.   III. Series.
    PS1545.D2Z65   1993
    813'.4—dc20   92-24231
                                                                CIP

The paper used in this publication meets the minimum requirements of
American National Standard for Information Sciences—Permanence of Paper
for Printed Library Materials. ANSI Z3948-1984.∞™

10 9 8 7 6 5 4 3 2 1

Printed in the United States of America

To our families

Contents

Preface

When Mary Mapes Dodge's novel *Hans Brinker; or, The Silver Skates*[1] was published in 1865, it became an immediate best-seller and has since acquired a life of its own in the popular imagination. Today Dodge is probably best known as the author of this beloved classic of children's literature. But a greater contribution to American cultural history was her influential work as editor of *St. Nicholas Magazine*[2] (1873–1905), during a period that has rightly been called a golden age of children's literature. She persuaded many of the most respected writers of her day to write for her readers, and taught them—when necessary—how to address an audience of children. For more than 30 years Dodge invited young America to enjoy the "pleasure ground"[3] she created for them. The pages of *St. Nicholas* during her term as editor remain today a treasury of good writing worth reading on its own merits and a valuable resource for the study of the changing culture of childhood in the late nineteenth century.

Yet surprisingly little serious critical attention has been paid to Dodge's role as a significant American writer, editor, and cultural gatekeeper. In this first full-length critical study of Dodge's work, it is our aim to describe and evaluate her achievement as a novelist, poet, journalist, and editor. In particular, we wish to direct attention to her special place in the network of writers and editors who transmitted the ideas of men and women of letters in New York and Boston to a wider audience. A great deal of basic research remains to be done on American periodical publishing for children, especially in terms of close studies of the work of individual editors. This book is intended to provide a useful foundation for future—and more detailed—work on Dodge's career and on the circle of men and women of letters whose work she promoted and helped to shape in the years 1873–1905.

Our account of Dodge's life in chapter 1 draws on a number of sources. Catharine Morris Wright's *Lady of the Silver Skates: The Life and Correspondence of Mary Mapes Dodge*,[4] a biography authorized by the Dodge family, was valuable to us especially for its excerpts from otherwise-unavailable family letters; for the convenience of readers, we have quoted letters from Wright's edition wherever possible. We profited also from a number of brief but vivid accounts of Dodge to be found in the memoirs and reminiscences of such friends and colleagues as Lu Runkle, Fayal Clarke, and Candace Wheeler. Any study of Dodge's life and work must begin with a survey of the abundant manuscript material carefully preserved by her family and her publishers. At Princeton University Library we examined family documents, photographs, and other memorabilia, as well as Dodge's personal and business correspondence. We also consulted the notebooks and correspondence of her nephew, Spencer Mapes, who in 1939 began to research a biography of Dodge that he never completed. His correspondence included interview material with Dodge's close associate, Fayal Clarke, and letters from some of the younger authors and staff with whom Dodge worked at *St. Nicholas*. Further insight into Dodge's relationships with friends and family members was provided by letters held in the collections of the Alderman Library at the University of Virginia, the de Grummond Collection at the McCain Library of the University of Southern Mississippi, the Huntington Library, the Stowe-Day Foundation in Hartford, Columbia University, and the Library of Congress.

In chapter 2 we present a selective study of Dodge's early journalism, which is of special importance for its exploration of some of the ideas and themes that preoccupied her throughout her career. At Princeton we were able to consult Dodge's own copy of the *United States Journal*, marked to indicate the pieces she wrote herself. Among Dodge's personal books were volumes of poetry and essays by her grandfather, Garrit Furman; in one of these we found a likely source for her essay on the "Insanity of Cain." Horace Scudder's notebooks and diaries at Harvard's Houghton

Library and Dodge's many letters to him, available at the Huntington Library, made clear his role as her literary mentor. Fragile copies of *Hearth and Home* held in the preservation department at Yale's Sterling Library demonstrated that Dodge's reputation as a lively, versatile, and extremely hardworking editor was well earned.

In chapters 3 and 6 we offer the first extensive studies of *The Irvington Stories*[5] and of Dodge's novel *Donald and Dorothy*.[6] The popularity of the stories when published says something of the taste of the 1860s. They present early treatments of some topics— play and Christmas—that were to become important in her later work and demonstrate many of her strengths and some of her weaknesses as a writer. A couple of stories—"Capt. George, the Drummer-Boy" and "Cushamee"—deserve to be better known, and we hope the attention given them here will bring them a wider reading.

Dodge's novel for older children, *Donald and Dorothy*, was extremely popular in its day, and Dodge herself was very fond of it. Though it never achieved the classic status of *Hans Brinker*, the story is valuable for its picture of upper-middle-class domestic life and for the questions it raises about the limitations of the world it describes. Letters in the Alderman Library of the University of Virginia, the Scribner Archive at Princeton, and the "Letter-Box" department of *St. Nicholas* itself were useful to us in clarifying Dodge's own feelings about the book as well as her assessment of her audience's reaction to it.

Our study of *Hans Brinker* in chapter 4 examines the novel's structure, symbolism, thematics, and narrative technique. We have benefited from the insights of Jerome Griswold in his article "*Hans Brinker*: Sunny World, Angry Waters,"[7] though our approach to the novel differs somewhat from his. We also discuss the story of the Hero of Haarlem, the little boy who put his finger in the dyke, establishing that this is not, as critics have contended, original with Dodge, but showing how it functions to bring her personal myth of courage and endurance home to even the youngest of her readers. We are indebted to a correspondent from New Zealand, Ralph R. Bodle, for information leading us to the versions of this story published in Beeton's *Boy's Own Magazine*[8] and *Old Merry's Annual*.[9] And we are grateful to librarians at Pace's Mortola Library, the Library of Congress, and Toronto Public Library's Osborne Collection for obtaining copies of this material for us.

In chapter 5 we look at Dodge's interest in games and play, which appeared in her many how-to pieces describing party games, in her book *A Few Friends and How They Amused Themselves*,[10] and in extended passages in both of her novels. We also look at Dodge's verse. Her serious poetic efforts are of interest because of their contemporary popularity and because of what they reveal of her personal concerns and religious attitudes. Her light verse for adults, mawkish when it deals with children from an adult perspective and lightly humorous when it deals with the follies of men and women in their social relations, is not in itself memorable. Her rhymes and jingles for children—often dashed off hastily while the presses waited—offered an amusing, updated "Mother Goose" for the late-nineteenth-century child. Dodge's correspondence with her publisher, in the Scribner Archive at Princeton, gave us some insight into her own feelings about her published poetry, as did a revealing letter to Henry Wadsworth Longfellow at the Houghton Library.

Anyone working on *St. Nicholas Magazine* will be grateful for the pioneering work of R. Gordon Kelly in the field of American children's periodicals. Both his *Mother Was a Lady*[11] and his *Children's Periodicals of the United States*[12] were useful to us. Fred Erisman's article on *St. Nicholas*[13] in Kelly's survey includes a good assessment of the magazine during Dodge's term as editor, and his unpublished dissertation, "There Was a Child Went Forth: A Study of *St. Nicholas Magazine* and Selected Children's Authors, 1890–1915,"[14] sets the work of several writers for *St. Nicholas* in the context of nineteenth-century American utopian thought. Mary June Roggenbuck's unpublished dissertation, "*St. Nicholas Magazine*: A Study of the Impact and Historical Influence of the Editorship of Mary Mapes Dodge,"[15] provides a convenient overview of the contents of the periodical while Dodge was in charge. Lawrence Fuller's paper "Mary Mapes Dodge and *St.*

Nicholas: The Development of a Philosophy and Practice of Publishing for Young People"[16] draws on a different array of correspondence from Wright (1979), notably on Dodge's letters to Horace Scudder. Wright's "How 'St. Nicholas' Got Rudyard Kipling: And What Happened Then"[17] included otherwise-unavailable letters from Kipling to Dodge.

Unlike her friend Horace Scudder, Dodge never wrote a book summing up her editorial philosophy and explaining her ideas about what makes for excellence in children's literature. But her personal and literary correspondence is full of practical criticism on work in hand. For chapters 7 and 8 we have mined Dodge's correspondence and the archives of her publishers for material that shows the editor in action, as it were. In the Century Company Archives at the New York Public Library, in the Scribner Archive at Princeton, and in the editorial correspondence of Dodge's assistant Fayal Clarke at the Alderman Library of the University of Virginia we found interoffice memos and detailed letters to authors that clarify the editorial standards of *St. Nicholas*. Comparative studies of material edited for *St. Nicholas* and versions of the same material in manuscript or hardcover also proved revealing. We were fortunate to be able to consult a manuscript copy of Kate Douglas Wiggin's *Polly Oliver's Problem*[18] at the Huntington Library and to get a photocopy of John Townsend Trowbridge's *His One Fault*[19] from the Beinecke Library. The Albert Bigelow Paine papers at the Huntington Library included a number of letters from children to the editor in charge of the St. Nicholas League. But, of course, our major resource has been the volumes of *St. Nicholas* itself, made available to us on loan from Yale and on microfilm in the Mortola Library at Pace.

In writing this book we have incurred debts to many people. At Pace University our work has been supported by summer research grants, travel grants, and library acquisitions. We are particularly grateful for the assistance of our provost, Joseph Pastore; Deans Joseph Houle and Charles Masiello of Dyson College; and Robert Klaeger, chair of the Department of Literature and Communications, Dyson College. For help in obtaining materials we are indebted to Noreen McGuire, Harriet Hwang, Robert Loomis, Eva knecht, Robert Dell, Phyllis Edelson, and Vicky Gannon at Pace; to the staff of the reference department at Duane Library of Fordham University; to Jean Preston at Princeton; to Dee Jones at the de Grummond Collection at Southern Mississippi; and to Suzanne Zaks at the Stowe-Day Foundation. Mitzi Myers and the Research Society for Victorian Periodicals made our first visit to the Huntington Library possible; Suzanne Rahn shared her insights into Dodge's editorial work with us most collegially; and Anne MacLeod offered counsel and help with medical research. We are grateful to them all.

Chronology

1831	Mary Elizabeth (Lizzie) Mapes born 26 January in New York City to James Jay and Sophie (Furman) Mapes.
1847	Family moves to Mapleridge, Waverly, New Jersey.
1850	Father founds the *Working Farmer*.
1851	Lizzie marries William Dodge.
1852	Son James (Jamie) born 20 June.
1855	Son Harrington (Harry) born 15 November.
1858	William dies. Lizzie returns to family home, Mapleridge, near Newark, New Jersey, with children.
1861	Dodge's father purchases the *United States Journal*. Dodge assists him in editorial work; begins to write for this and other publications.
1863	Begins to contribute adult stories to *Harper's New Monthly Magazine*.
1864	*Irvington Stories*.
1865	*Hans Brinker; or, The Silver Skates*.
1866	Father dies.
1867	Dodge becomes contributor to Horace E. Scudder's *Riverside Magazine for Young People*.
1868	*A Few Friends and How They Amused Themselves*. Becomes associate editor of *Hearth and Home*, to which she contributes through 1873.

1871   "Miss Malony on the Chinese Question" in *Scribner's Monthly*. Begins using the name Mary Mapes Dodge professionally.

1873   Publishes (anonymously) in July issue of *Scribner's Monthly* a statement of principles on which *St. Nicholas* will be guided. Founds *St. Nicholas*, with Frank R. Stockton as assistant editor. Dodge visits Europe in May and meets many literary figures, including Lewis Carroll and George MacDonald. Scribner's reissues *Hans Brinker* in a revised edition with a new preface.

1874   Moves to New York City. *Hans Brinker* is published in a French edition that wins a prize from the French Academy. *Rhymes and Jingles*.

1876   Sister Louise dies. "The Two Mysteries" (poem). *Theophilus and Others*.

1877   *Baby Days: A Selection of Songs, Stories, and Pictures, for Very Little Folks*. Frank R. Stockton resigns as assistant editor of *St. Nicholas* and is replaced by William Fayal Clarke.

1878   Dodge visits sister Kate in San Francisco. Meets Kate Douglas Wiggin and Helen Hunt Jackson.

1879   *Along the Way* (verse).

1880   Becomes seriously ill. Loses property at Waverly, New Jersey, because of financial reverses.

1881   Son Harry dies.

1881–1882 *Donald and Dorothy* serialized in *St. Nicholas*.

1884   Mother dies. *Baby World*.

1888   Purchases Yarrow Cottage, Onteora, New York.

1894   *The Land of Pluck. When Life Is Young* (verse).

1897   *A New Baby World*.

1898   Compiles *The Children's Book of Recitations*. Revises and reissues *The Irvington Stories*. Visits Europe. Sister Sophie dies.

1899   Albert Bigelow Paine begins the St. Nicholas League.

1904   *Rhymes and Jingles* (enlarged edition). *Poems and Verses* (about two-thirds have appeared in *Along the Way*).

1905   Dies 21 August at Onteora, New York.

Subsequent History of *St. Nicholas*

1905   Fayal Clarke becomes editor.

1927   Fayal Clarke retires.

1930   Century Company sells *St. Nicholas*.

1940   *St. Nicholas* ceases publication.

1943   *St. Nicholas* revived for three issues.

1

MMD: The Life

Mary Mapes Dodge (1831–1905) is best known today for her novel *Hans Brinker; or, The Silver Skates: A Story of Life in Holland*, a children's classic that is still selling well in many editions and six languages (Wright 1979, 32). But in her own time she was better known as the editor of what has often been called the best of all children's magazines, *St. Nicholas*. From 1873 until her death in 1905, Dodge conducted the journal that she called a "pleasure ground" for children ("CM," 353), and "with the opening issues, the child-readers of the country recognized that they had come into their own at last," for the new monthly was "a rich mine" of "entertaining reading fitted with wonderful skill" to their tastes and needs.[1]

Dodge arrived on the New York literary scene at a time when changing attitudes toward children and their books had created a climate in which a child-centered kind of writing could find an audience. The reading public was expanding, and new printing technology had made it possible for publishers to produce magazines and books of graphic excellence and still maintain a profit. The instability of the economy and the rapidity of social and political change had raised new challenges to old values. Many middle-class parents were eager to expand their children's cultural horizons, yet wanted to ground them in traditional values. When Roswell Smith, Josiah G. Holland, and Charles Scribner wanted

1

an editor for the ideal children's magazine to accompany their own *Scribner's Monthly* into the homes of America's genteel middle class, they turned naturally to Dodge, an established writer for children who had made a great success of the children's pages of *Hearth and Home*, and offered her the editorship of the magazine she would name *St. Nicholas*.

Dodge, who had learned the delicate art of literary networking at her father's knee, was never happier than when in the middle of a busy and creative social whirl. As an active member of the influential circle of writers, artists, and intellectual leaders associated with *Scribner's Monthly* (later the *Century*) and *St. Nicholas*, she seems to have known just about everyone in New York's literary establishment. Few of her friends and acquaintances seemed able to resist her demands that they address the young readers of *St. Nick*. Over the years, contributors included people like Louisa May Alcott, Thomas Bailey Aldrich, L. Frank Baum, Frances Hodgson Burnett, Rudyard Kipling, Henry Wadsworth Longfellow, Thomas Nelson Page, Theodore Roosevelt, Christina Rossetti, Frank Stockton, Horace Scudder, Robert Louis Stevenson, Alfred, Lord Tennyson, Mark Twain, and Kate Douglas Wiggin.

Sensitive to the needs of her audience and possessed of an unusual ability to convey those needs to writers and artists, Dodge was able to produce, for more than 30 years, a magazine of unmatched excellence. She became, like her colleague, *Century* editor Richard Watson Gilder, an important cultural gatekeeper, her work at *St. Nicholas* extending Scribner and Company's mission of cultural uplift and moral reform to what she always insisted was a uniquely important audience: America's children, and their parents and teachers.

To appreciate the nature of Dodge's influence on American children and their literature, it is necessary to look closely at her own education and at her work as a journalist, writer, and editor. Reflecting on the goals Dodge had set for *St. Nicholas* in a retrospective piece he wrote for the magazine's fiftieth anniversary, her associate editor and successor, Fayal Clarke, noted that the magazine was to give pleasure, yet be instructive, and to build character, cultivate the imagination, and stimulate ambition for a life of service, yet somehow prepare children for "life as it is."[2] These principles, with their bold mixture of idealism and practicality, were the foundation of Dodge's program for young readers. The story of how she came to hold them and how her work influenced the lives of three generations of American children begins with the family life and education that gave her both her sense of mission and the ability to carry it out.

Early Life

Mary Elizabeth Mapes was born to Sophia Furman and James Jay Mapes on 26 January in New York City. The year was probably 1831.[3] When Mary Elizabeth—or Lizzie, as everyone called her—was born, the family lived at 32 Greenwich Street, near the tip of Manhattan Island. An older sister, Marie Louise, and a younger sister, Sophie, were close enough in age to be companions and playmates. Later, after the Mapeses had moved uptown to Reade Street, two more children, Charley and Kate, were born. The Furman and Mapes families had been prominent in New York for several generations. Dodge's maternal grandfather, Judge Garrit Furman, owned an estate at Maspeth, Long Island, and had an interest in a farmer's market in New York City. Furman was a man of literary interests who wrote charming essays for a Long Island newspaper and published a book of poetry and a lively historical novel.

The Furman and Mapes families had been friends and neighbors, and so Dodge's parents knew each other from childhood. Her paternal grandfather, General Jonas Mapes, had fought in the American Revolution and was a personal friend of the Marquis de Lafayette. The Mapes family were merchant tailors, but James Jay Mapes was interested in science and journalism rather than commerce. He became an accomplished self-taught chemist, agricultural expert, inventor, editor, and publisher. Mapes was a tireless worker for the cause of agricultural reform and a recognized leader in intellectual circles in New York and Philadelphia.

He taught at the National Academy of Design and edited the *American Repertory of Arts, Sciences, and Manufactures*. None of these activities brought in much money, however, and his "only dependable income came from the law courts, where he served as an expert witness in the field of patent litigation" (Wright 1979, 3). But he was a man of ideas, a brilliant talker, a wonderful storyteller, and something of a wit. His household was a meeting place for "men of science, poets, painters, musicians, statesmen, philosophers, journalists."[4] And the five surviving Mapes children grew up in an atmosphere that was itself a "liberal education" (Runkle, 277).

Dodge's own reminiscences were of "a devoted father and mother and a happy childhood, a remarkably happy childhood, watched over with loving care" (Clarke 1905, 1060). The Mapes children were educated at home by a governess who taught them languages, including French and Latin, and trained them in music and drawing. Their father, who believed the juvenile literature of the time to be a dreary "wasteland" (Runkle, 277), introduced his children to a wide range of literature, including "the Bible, the old English ballads, Shakspere, Milton, Bunyan, and Walter Scott" (Clarke 1905, 1060). Lizzie was exceptionally talented. Before the age of 10 she had become an avid reader, and was known in the family for "poetical effusions" on family anniversaries, some of which she used to "repeat with gleeful amusement in after years" (Clarke 1905, 1060). But it became clear quite early that she was also gifted with "an aptitude for music, drawing, and modelling, a quick ear and tongue for languages, a clear and critical judgment, great executive capacity, and an indomitable cheerfulness and serenity of spirit, which made any labor or success seem possible to her" (Runkle, 278). By the time she was in her teens, Lizzie's ability to write clear, effective prose made her a valued assistant to her learned father in the preparation of his many pamphlets and articles.

James Jay Mapes—inventor, writer, editor, scientist, agricultural reformer—was a natural teacher with a restless urge to share his often-controversial ideas with a wide public. Among the ideas Mapes held in advance of his time was the notion that chemical fertilizers could be made to enrich soils and that the application of careful scientific research to the practical work of farming could revolutionize American agriculture. To test and demonstrate his ideas, Mapes—never averse to precipitate action when in the grip of one of his enthusiasms—decided to buy a worn-out farm that he could transform into a model property. With the help of a young friend, Mapes was able to purchase the land he wanted, and moved his family to Mapleridge, in Waverly, New Jersey, near Newark.

Mapes's financial affairs involved many intricate and not-always-straightforward deals with friends and associates. The friend on whom he relied to buy Mapleridge was a young lawyer named William Dodge. Dodge had earned an M.A. from Columbia and, like Mapes, was a member of the St. Nicholas Society, a social club whose membership was reserved to descendants of persons resident in New York City in the eighteenth century. When Mapes first brought Dodge home to meet his family, the open-faced, fair-haired young man was 32 and Mapes's daughter Lizzie was a lively and attractive 19-year-old.

Married Life

In 1851, when she was 20, William Dodge and Lizzie Mapes married, and the young couple went to live with William's family in New York City. They appear to have been happy together. Dodge some years later confided to her friend Lu Runkle that she felt William had helped her to grow intellectually. The "Theophilus" sketches she was later to write about the young married life of a New York couple are affectionate and humorous, and seem to be based in part on her own experience during these years. If so, the sketches suggest that the Dodges may well have had a warm relationship with a great deal of easy give-and-take.

In June 1852 the Dodges' first son, James Mapes, was born. In 1855 William went to France to supervise the delivery of America's exhibits at the International Exhibition, afterward visiting Holland, Belgium, Germany, and Switzerland. And soon after his return from Europe the couple's second son, Harrington Mapes, was born. By 1857 it was clear that the young Dodges had become inextricably involved in James Mapes's complicated financial dealings. Mapes had not only borrowed money from Dodge to buy the Mapleridge property but also mortgaged and remortgaged it to purchase more and more adjacent land. When, in August 1857, the securities market fell, Mapes was put under extra pressure. He tried to arrange a scheme whereby young Dodge would go to Europe to introduce and sell patents for a new buttonhole machine, Dodge's share of the profits to go to Mapes. But the plan required an investment in the expenses of the trip, and Dodge's approach to a potential sponsor—his friend Nelson Chase's mother-in-law, Madame Jumel—failed (Wright 1979, 13–14).

The year 1857 was an unusually difficult one for William Dodge, the failure of the buttonhole-machine scheme being only the first of a series of disasters. By September 1857 James Jay Mapes was supposed to have repaid William $2,900 in cash—all the rent he owed, with interest—and to have assumed the burden of the various mortgages that had been taken out against the property; however, he was apparently unable to do any of this (Wright 1979, 10, 17). To add to the emotional impact of his financial reverses, "In October, the Crystal Palace, which the city had taken over in receivership and given into the hands of the American Institute with James Jay still vice president and William Dodge his active assistant, burned to the ground. The steam calliope played 'Pop Goes the Weasel' until the dome exploded and fell in" (Wright 1979, 14). Moreover, to all of this was added the serious illness of Jamie Dodge, then six, who was diagnosed as suffering from an incurable bleeding from the sinus, "purpurea haemmoragica," which appeared to threaten the boy with death, or at best a life of invalidism (Wright 1979, 14). Depressed and perhaps upset by his son's condition, William Dodge left his home to take a walk late in the afternoon of 28 October 1858 and never returned.

The concern of his family at this unexplained disappearance was evidenced in a series of newspaper advertisements placed in the *New York Times* in the succeeding days, requesting information about a middle-aged man thought to be wandering about

"under the influence it is supposed of melancholy or monomania."[5]
A body identified as Dodge's was recovered, and a funeral was held
on 11 November, 15 days after his disappearance. The records in
the Brooklyn cemetery where the body was buried indicate that
the cause of death was drowning and give as the date of death 28
October 1858, the day he left home (Wright 1979, 16).

Although Mary Mapes Dodge and her family maintained a dignified and unbroken silence about the circumstances of William's
disappearance and death, certain passages in her poetry suggest
that she had to struggle long and hard to achieve peace of mind
and spiritual poise in the face of an agonizing personal loss. And
an oblique reference in a letter from her friend Robert Dale Owen
hints that she might have spoken to him of the bond she had felt
with her husband and her feelings when he died. Moved by the
"beautiful heart-history" of her marriage, Owen wrote to her: "I
conceive the blank darkness after seven years of genial light; &
yet I hold you to have been 'blessed among women.' For that which
has occurred—happiness that has been enjoyed—cannot perish."[6]

Nevertheless, Dodge's life was now irrevocably changed. She
was a widow with two young children to support and, thanks to
her father's irresponsibility, not in a very strong financial position.
But determined to do her best for her family, she left her in-
laws' New York City home and returned to Mapleridge. Here she
devoted herself to the education of her two young sons, Jamie and
Harry. Dodge's closest woman friend, Lucia Gilbert Runkle, wrote
that at this time Dodge resolved "to take up her life again in the
old spirit of rejoicing; to rear and educate her boys as their father
would have done; to do a man's work with the persistent application and faithfulness of a man, to gain a man's pay, yet to leave
herself freedom and freshness to enter into all her children's interests and pursuits as their comrade and friend" (Runkle, 280–81).
Many visitors to Mapleridge have described the way Dodge took
over the upper floor of one of the farm's outbuildings to create a
"den" where she could retire to write and think without being too
far from the boys, who turned the lower floor of the same building
into a gymnasium and a studio where they ran an amateur printing press.

Dodge plunged into the work of educating her children with enthusiasm and total commitment: "She flew kites with them, skated with them, swam with them, passed hours in their improvised gymnasium, set up many a 'form' at the printing-press, tramped miles beside them, collecting specimens for microscope or herbarium. Whatever subject interested them she studied in secret . . . the crystallization of iron, the effects of heat and cold, the laws of statics and dynamics . . . the science and art of music" (Runkle, 292–93).

Early Editorial Work

In 1851 James Jay Mapes had purchased a magazine, the *Working Farmer*, that he used to popularize his ideas about innovative approaches to agriculture. After his graduation from Harvard, Mapes's enterprising son Charley entered the fertilizer business and by January 1858 had also become assistant editor of the *Working Farmer*; in 1859 he took over its publication. After the death of William Dodge, when Lizzie had also returned to the family home at Mapleridge, James Mapes decided to expand his efforts "in order to meet the requirements of a more varied class of readers" (quoted in Wright 1979, 24). He purchased the *United States Journal* and made Lizzie, at 28, its editor. James Mapes had found in his second daughter a natural writer whose talent emerged early and developed quickly. Dodge's editorial apprenticeship under her father was an extension of the learning and doing that had characterized her upbringing from the earliest days. And since James Mapes, gifted as he was, lacked managerial finesse, Dodge's quick mind and executive ability made her an ideal editorial collaborator. The two magazines were published together, the *Working Farmer* offering practical advice on agricultural matters and the *United States Journal* offering cultural enrichment with poems, stories, reviews, and articles of general interest.

The collaborative family atmosphere in which this first editorial effort was carried on may well have established the pattern that

Dodge was later to follow at *St. Nicholas*. Working with her father to disseminate his ideas on farming and to bring her readers up to date on cultural matters, Dodge learned to see editorial work as essentially educational. She became adept at shaping researched material on a great variety of subjects into readable notes and articles that were appealing as well as instructive, a skill she was to put to good use throughout her writing career.

Early Writing

The Irvington Stories

Aside from work for her father's periodicals, Dodge also wrote essays and stories for other leading magazines of the day, and "the periodicals to which she sent even her earliest manuscripts accepted them all and eagerly asked for more" (Clarke 1905, 1062). But on 14 May 1864 Dodge moved into a different field. James Jay Mapes wrote to his daughter from New York that publisher James O'Kane wanted a book "for boys from 8 or 10 to 18 years of age." Mapes suggested that the book might deal with the Civil War, which was then in progress: "Enlist a youngster and carry him through this war, make him smart, of course."[7] This hint was the seed of "Capt. George, the Drummer-Boy," one of the most successful of Dodge's stories. Mapes added the welcome news that O'Kane liked what he'd read of her work and that he would be interested in having Dodge do a series of volumes for him.

The book Dodge wrote for O'Kane, *The Irvington Stories*, appeared in November of the same year. Though not a best-seller, the collection of stories went through several editions quickly enough to establish O'Kane's confidence in Dodge's ability to appeal to her chosen audience. The *North American Review* noted that Dodge's stories were neither prosy nor "sermons in words of two syllables." In them the reviewer saw "what is gracious and lovely in childhood" "appealed to indirectly, with something of motherly tenderness in the tone" (quoted in Runkle, 285).

Hans Brinker; or, The Silver Skates

The success of *The Irvington Stories* led its publisher to ask Dodge for another series of stories. But she was already at work on a longer narrative, a story she had been improvising for her sons. Fascinated by Motley's *The Rise of the Dutch Republic*[8] and *The History of the United Netherlands*,[9] she made the locale of this story Holland and determined to include in it as much Dutch history and background color as possible. The result was not the sort of book O'Kane wanted or expected from Dodge; however, because her first book had been so successful, he decided to chance publication, and *Hans Brinker; or, The Silver Skates* appeared in 1865. The book made publishing history: it received excellent reviews and immediately became a best-seller. *Harper's* described it as "a pleasant story, wrought out in all its details with the minuteness of a Dutch painting, of life in Holland in the olden time."[10] And the *Nation*, noting that Dodge's earlier writing for the young had demonstrated "a very rare ability to meet their wants," observed that she had done "nothing better than this charming tale, alive with incident and action, adorned rather than freighted with useful facts, and moral without moralization."[11] Compared with the scale of its later sales, this first burst of popularity appears modest in retrospect. The book really came into its own a few years later, when it was reissued by Scribner's and translated into many languages, including Dutch.

The Literary Life

Shortly after the publication of *Hans Brinker*, James Jay Mapes died, "stricken mounting the Court House steps in New York" (Wright 1979, 36). Despite the financial muddles and debts he left behind, his was a presence that was much missed. In March 1866 Robert Dale Owen appeared at Mapleridge to offer condolences to Sophia and her family. This former diplomat, social reformer, and man of letters had been a friend of James Jay Mapes. His letters to Dodge show him to have been a sentimental, emotional man whose old-fashioned gallantry could become a bit tedious; nevertheless, Dodge found him a valuable ally whose fatherly presence seems to have brightened a difficult time in her life. Owen introduced Dodge to many of the people he knew in the New York literary world, people like Phoebe and Alice Cary, at whose salon the young woman encountered celebrities from the worlds of literature, politics, and journalism. There Dodge met many people with whom she would develop future editorial relationships— Thomas Bailey Aldrich and John Greenleaf Whittier, for example—and she met Lucia Gilbert Calhoun (later Runkle), an intelligent and talented journalist who would become the closest of Dodge's many accomplished women friends.

Just before Christmas in 1866, Dodge had another visitor at Mapleridge: a personable young man named Horace Scudder who had just been asked by Hurd and Houghton to edit a new children's periodical for them. His ideas about writing for children were congenial with Dodge's, and the two became good friends. Although Dodge wrote a series of original and entertaining short pieces about party games and amusements for Scudder's *Riverside Magazine for Young People*, perhaps the most important outcome of this meeting is to be found in the correspondence, in which these two enormously influential editors shared ideas about the practical work of editing and writing for children.

The pieces Dodge wrote for Scudder on games, toys, and home amusements were well received, and he wanted more. She, however, had another project in mind, which turned into her third book, *A Few Friends and How They Amused Themselves* (1868). Dodge, who had copyrighted a game called "The Protean Cards," had always been fascinated by game-playing. Like many families of the day, the Mapeses had been accustomed to simple home entertainment in the evening, and throughout her life she continued to be a popular hostess who always had something fresh and new for her guests to do, see, or enjoy. *A Few Friends* described the effect of participation in a series of elaborate party games on a group of adult New Yorkers who meet at one another's homes during the social season.

In 1868 Dodge accepted a position as associate editor responsible for "Home and Miscellany" (which include a juvenile department) at a new magazine called *Hearth and Home*, under coeditors Harriet Beecher Stowe and Donald G. Mitchell ("Ik Marvel"). Dodge worked hard at *Hearth and Home*, doing much of the practical, day-to-day editorial work for Stowe, an absentee editor. Here Dodge began to exercise her talents for wheedling contributions out of well-known authors, beginning with her father's old friend William Cullen Bryant. And here too she met a man who was destined to become one of her most trusted colleagues and best friends—Frank R. Stockton, whom she hired as an assistant in 1870 after Stowe and Mitchell had left. Although Dodge's work on *Hearth and Home* was very successful, she never had complete editorial freedom there, and when something better appeared on the horizon, she was not sorry to leave.

St. Nicholas: The Early Years

Dodge's editorial work had attracted the attention of three men with whose publishing ventures her name was to be closely linked: Charles Scribner, Josiah Holland, and Roswell Smith. Scribner was head of the distinguished publishing house that bore his name and publisher of a magazine called *Hours at Home*; Holland had been a doctor and a journalist and was now a best-selling author whose *Timothy Titcomb* had been a lucrative property for Scribner's firm; and Smith was a businessman and financier. Holland had met Smith in Switzerland and proposed to him that they combine their efforts to publish a new magazine. When they returned to New York, they offered Charles Scribner 40 percent of the stock of their new enterprise—Charles Scribner and Company—keeping 60 percent for themselves. Scribner decided to merge *Hours at Home* with the new publication, and *Scribner's Monthly* was born.

When Scribner first began *Hours at Home*, he had wanted Holland to edit it; when Holland declined, Scribner had turned to Dodge's old friend from Newark, Richard Watson Gilder. Now Gilder was to assist Holland in editing *Scribner's Monthly*, and one of his first acts was to enlist Dodge as a contributor, beginning with a substantial article, for the very first issue, about the New York Juvenile Asylum.

By 1872 Dodge was in the pleasant position of considering an offer of the editorship of *Hearth and Home* when Roswell Smith asked her to send him a letter outlining her ideas about a children's magazine. When she did, Smith was so impressed by the result that he sent a check by return mail and kept the manuscript for publication in *Scribner's Magazine.* (Wright 1979, 69).

Soon after, Dodge was asked by Smith, Josiah Gilbert, and Charles Scribner to create for them the very sort of children's periodical she had described in her piece, which had been published in their magazine, *Scribner's Monthly* ("CM," 352–54). The decision to accept the offer was not easy, for Dodge had other ambitions: her writing for adults had been well received, and she wanted to try writing novels. According to her colleague Fayal Clarke, however, Dodge's sense of duty told her that plenty of people were writing for adults but no one was doing what she knew she could do for children (Clarke 1905, 1063).

Dodge left *Hearth and Home* on 27 March 1873 and in April entered the employ of Scribner and Company, bringing with her the reliable and congenial Frank Stockton to serve as assistant editor and hold the fort in New York while Dodge slipped off to Europe for a much-needed vacation. Jamie, having just graduated from Rutgers, had a new job to occupy him, but Harry, who had been ill and needed a rest, was free to accompany his mother to England and the Netherlands. Aboard the SS *Calabria*, the Dodges met author George MacDonald and his family, and the two families hit it off so well that the Dodges were invited to stay with the MacDonalds in England. There Dodge saw her English publishers; met Dante Gabriel and Christina Rossetti, Lewis Carroll, and Jean Ingelow; and became acquainted with many influential figures in the publishing world, persons to whom she had been given letters of introduction by the people at Scribner's (Wright 1979, 78).

By the time Dodge returned to New York, the Panic of 1873 had begun, and though there was reason to fear its impact on the publishing world, Scribner and Company pressed forward boldly

with its new project. The company had earlier absorbed Scudder's
Riverside Magazine and now took the opportunity to buy out another important competitor, John Townsend Trowbridge's *Our
Young Folks*, published in Boston by Ticknor and Fields. Because
it was only good business to ensure that the audience for *Our
Young Folks* carried over to *St. Nicholas*, Smith, Holland, and
Dodge made every effort to conciliate Trowbridge, who felt keenly
the loss of his editorial position. They moved up the proposed first
issue of their new journal so as to have a smoother transition, and
they persuaded Trowbridge to become a regular contributor.

The press hailed the new journal as a unique achievement in
"all the history of American periodical literature"—"a success
fairly won by the taste and judgment of the editors, who clearly
understand what children like and what it is well for them to
have, and by the liberality of the publishers, who rightly believe
that children are entitled to just as much consideration as grown
folks, and have spared no pains to make their magazine in every
way attractive."[12] In the first few years of her editorship, Dodge
set up the format of the journal and acquired a stellar network of
contributors. During these years *St. Nicholas* also absorbed a
number of other juvenile periodicals. And by 1881 the Century
Company was formed by Smith and Holland to publish *Century
Magazine* and *St. Nicholas*.

One of the most important things Dodge did in her first years
at *St. Nicholas* was to draw her readers into a close-knit group by
encouraging their participation in the magazine and offering them
the sense of empowerment that came with having their thoughts
on significant matters heeded. The "Letter-Box" featured letters
from readers; "Jack-in-the-Pulpit," Dodge's own personal column,
invited readers to ask and answer questions; and the "St. Nicholas
League" offered readers a chance to have their contributions published in the magazine.

Dodge worked extremely hard, but "all her conscientious labor
was heartily seconded by her generous publishers." Dodge herself
said of Roswell Smith that he was "ambitious for the work in
hand, rather than for himself. He counted no cost too great for

the carrying out of a plan; and the success of ST. NICHOLAS . . . rested upon his energy and liberality" (Clarke 1905, 1064).

In 1874 Dodge published a collection of sprightly little verses meant to amuse and entertain children. This was the first in a series of compilations she would put together through the years. She became expert at recycling her published verse and stories for children into small books that sold well. *Rhymes and Jingles*,[13] in a number of editions, was in print for many years. In 1873 Scribner, Armstrong also acquired the rights to *Hans Brinker* and over the next few years put out several editions. The publisher's interest in promoting the book, together with its author's new celebrity, revived *Hans Brinker's* reputation and helped to ensure the book's status as a children's classic. In 1875 a French translation of *Hans Brinker*—published together with a version of *Little Women*—received a prize from the French Academy, and the next few years brought foreign editions in England, France, Holland, and Italy (Wright 1979, 91).

When, however, Dodge in 1876 published a selected collection of her essays for adults, the book, despite a glowing review in *Scribner's Monthly*, did not sell as well as she and Scribner's had hoped. *Theophilus and Others*[14] was one of her own favorite books, and it is clear from the many letters she wrote to Charles Scribner on the subject that she took its failure to heart.

In the 1870s Dodge's family had left Mapleridge and settled in New York City, where Dodge and her boys took rooms in a boardinghouse. Such places offered convenient and comfortable, if somewhat cramped, accommodations. To these quarters Dodge drew a lively set of writers and fellow editors who flocked to her informal evenings "at home" as happily as in later and more affluent days they would come to receptions at any of her spacious apartments near Central Park. Dodge's mother and her widowed sister Sophie boarded elsewhere in New York, while her sister Louise was taken to Charleston, where it was thought the mild climate would help her consumption. In June 1876 Louise died, and it is likely that her sister's death occasioned the writing of Dodge's most celebrated poem for adults, "The Two Mysteries."

This poem, published in *Scribner's Monthly* in October 1876, attracted a great deal of attention and praise, perhaps as much for its theme as for its merit as a poem. But in her own day this was one of Dodge's most famous works, and it brought her a great many letters from readers who felt consoled by its earnest expression of simple faith.

In 1877 Frank Stockton resigned as assistant editor and was replaced by William Fayal Clarke. Dodge's brother Charley wrote to their sister Kate describing Lizzie's despair at the loss of Stockton, her "right-hand man," but noting that after a brief trial, Clarke had proved "to be an 'angel and a trump' so Liz is all smiles & in hopes again."[15] Dodge's hopes were well justified, for Clarke faithfully served *St. Nicholas* as her assistant editor for 28 years, and carried on Dodge's work as editor for 32 years after that. When he came to *St. Nicholas*, he was only 19, close to her son Harry's age. The Dodge boys liked Clarke at once, and he in effect became a part of Dodge's family, living in the household for more than 20 years.

In 1878 Dodge did a good bit of traveling. She visited her sister Kate in San Francisco, stopping in Colorado to see Helen Hunt Jackson, and while traveling back through Chicago to New York, she and her elder son, Jamie, met his future wife, Josephine Kern, on the train. The train stopped in a field of pink clover; Jamie picked some and asked his mother to give it to the pretty girl who had caught his eye. Since she was on her way to Europe, Jamie had to woo his bride-to-be by mail. But he was a determined young man who knew what he wanted, and his courtship was eventually successful.

In 1879 Dodge brought out a volume of verse called *Along the Way*.[16] It included her famous poem on life and death, "The Two Mysteries," as well as poems celebrating nature, such as "In the Cañon" and "Emerson." Many of the poems were published here for the first time; others had appeared in magazines; and a few, which she thought likely to appeal to adults as well as younger readers, were reprinted from an earlier anthology of verse for children.

Dodge's son Harry had worked for Scribner's briefly in 1879, but eyestrain apparently made it impossible for him to remain there. He tried but failed at another job, and took time out to nurse his mother when she suffered a fall while summering in the Adirondacks that year. At the time, Dodge wrote her son Jamie that Harry was "dreadfully low spirited . . . because he was not taking his part in the world and hadn't strength enough to fill any position or undertake any course of study."[17] In September 1879 Harry contracted typhoid, and his recovery was slow during the ensuing winter. By March, however, he was again sick, with what his mother termed in a letter to her sister Kate "Harry's terrible second illness which seemed . . . worse than the first because it threatened to sap his health for life."[18] This illness seems to have been psychological. In March 1880 Dodge complained in a letter to Jamie that "the hardest part of Harry's illness seems to be that I excite him. He feels that I may be overtaxed, etc., and the doctor makes me keep out of sight as much as possible."[19] By May Harry seemed better to his mother, though she worried that "his bodily strength had been slow in coming,"[20] and by midsummer Harry was working for his uncle Charley and earning a small salary. His mental condition, however, seemed to fluctuate from day to day (Wright 1979, 120). Accordingly, his uncle Charley took him to the Hartford Retreat, where he died, suddenly, in February 1881, of "congestion of the brain."[21] Shortly after Harry's death, Dodge went to visit Jamie and his wife and new baby, Kern. The new baby was a delight, but, though Dodge knew she must "try to be happy alone," it was difficult to do so. She wrote to Kate, "If I felt older it would be easier, for I long for their fresh young companionship that was so precious to me in the years that went so soon. We were like a sister & her brothers in those days—and it still could be so if we were together."[22] Dodge took the death of her younger son very much to heart, though she seems to have tried to come to terms with it. Fayal Clarke reported that she once said, " 'I had to give up one of my boys,' and added, in the same tender tone: 'but I don't think God feels about death as we do' " (Clarke 1905, 1070).

In 1881–82 Dodge's novel for older children, *Donald and Dorothy*, was published. The story combined a bit of mystery and adventure with an affectionate picture of domestic life. It was well received by readers but never achieved the classic status of *Hans Brinker*. Dodge's personal unhappiness during this period seems to have spilled over into her relationship with the patient and courteous Charles Scribner, son of Holland and Smith's partner, who had died in 1871. Scribner, unwilling to accede to her demands concerning contractual matters, lost *Donald and Dorothy* to Thomas Niles at Roberts Brothers of Boston. The negotiations over the rights to the novel delayed its publication and lost Dodge the benefit of the publicity attendant on the novel's publication as a serial in *St. Nicholas*. The book remained one of Dodge's favorites, even though its sales were disappointing.

Dodge had inherited nothing but debts from her father, and the first 15 years of her working life had been financially unrewarding. Now at last she was making a good income, but the economic climate of the 1870s and 1880s was full of uncertainty. Something of her attitude toward money matters is reflected in a piece she asked Elizabeth Stuart Phelps to write for *St. Nicholas* about a year after she wrote *Donald and Dorothy*. The article argued that every young woman—no matter how financially secure her life might seem—should "make herself mistress of some industry, or art, or profession, or trade" that would give her an independent means of livelihood. Phelps told Dodge's readers that rather than becoming dependent on others for their support, "it is honester, safer, nobler, and more womanly for a woman to be able to care for herself and for the father, or mother, or brother, or husband, or child, whom a hundred chances may, at any hour, fling upon her warm heart and brave hand for protection."[23]

St. Nicholas: The Middle Years

The period 1882–93 saw a new group of contributors coming to the fore at *St. Nicholas*. Richard Harding Davis, whose mother had written for Dodge, now himself entered the ranks of *St. Nicholas* contributors. Clever light verse by John Kendrick Bangs, Laura E. Richards, and *St. Nicholas* staffer Tudor Jenks began to appear. Palmer Cox wrote and illustrated a series of Brownie stories that became extremely popular (and made him a fortune). Such distinguished writers for adults as Edward Everett Hale, John Burroughs, William Dean Howells, and critic E. C. Stedman were persuaded to write for Mrs. Dodge's young readers. And Dodge, always eager to extend the readership of her magazine, tried to attract boys who liked action and adventure by printing the work of Mayne Reid and Joaquin Miller. Like the *Century*, *St. Nicholas* featured the work of a number of southern writers, two of whom—Joel Chandler Harris and Thomas Nelson Page—wrote stories rich in local color. And, of course, it was during these years that Dodge attracted to her magazine such international stars as Frances Hodgson Burnett, Rudyard Kipling, and Mark Twain.

The work style Dodge developed at Mapleridge carried over into her later editorial work. She made a pleasant, homelike environment of the offices of *St. Nicholas*, where the close-knit staff became like an extended family. And her own home served both as a social center for cultivating friendships with co-workers and potential contributors to *St. Nicholas* and as a busy office where she did much of her work. Though bringing work home was one of the secrets of Dodge's success, the practice had its drawbacks. Sometimes, especially in times of stress or illness, she took on more than she could handle, and there was no way of getting away from the details of her editorial task save by leaving New York altogether.

Dodge was supported, however, by a network of helpful friends, many of them prominent professional women, writers, and journalists. Among those closest to her were Lucia Gilbert Runkle, Helen Hunt Jackson, Kate Field, Libby Custer, and Ruth McEnery Stuart. But Dodge also moved in a wider circle of influential New Yorkers interested in politics, literature, and the arts. When Annie Nathan Meyer was trying to persuade the board of trustees of Columbia College that they should establish some provision for the education of women, it was to Dodge that she came for help. Dodge welcomed Meyer "warmly" and gave her "much excellent advice," as well as seeing to it that she met "the women most likely to be interested in a scheme for starting a college for women in New York."[24] Dodge helped to write the "Memorial" that persuaded the Columbia board of trustees to go ahead with the plan, and though she declined to become a trustee of Barnard College when it was founded, she remained a supporter of the institution and its work (Meyer, 91).

In 1885 Dodge's mother, Sophia Furman Mapes, died, and in 1891 the family suffered a particularly painful loss in the accidental drowning of her brother Charley's young son Bert. Dodge said of this incident that it "seemed to open all the wounds of my life" (quoted Wright 1979, 172). Here was the sudden death of a young man of her Harry's generation; moreover, because Bert's body was not recovered for some days, the whole situation was also reminiscent of the circumstances of William Dodge's death.

The Onteora Years

In the middle 1880s Dodge's own health became uncertain, though she was characteristically able to summon enormous energy when it was needed to perform some special task. In 1886 Dodge, who had been suffering from "ague, chill, and eye inflammation" and wrote "to her friend Lucy Morse that her 'special tyrants' were 'nerves, backbone & bronchial tubes,' "[25] was ordered by her doctor to take a trip to Europe for her health. While there, she met Candace Wheeler, who was in the process of setting up a summer colony in the Catskill Mountains for artists and literary people from New York. In 1888 Dodge bought a cottage at Onteora and from this time forward spent long summers there each year. Mark Twain, Richard Watson Gilder, Laurence Hutton, Brander Matthews, Maude Adams, and such old friends as Lu Runkle, Sarah C. Woolsey, Kate Field, Ruth McEnery Stuart, and Libbie Custer formed there a social circle as dazzling as might have been found in a New York salon. But the atmosphere at Onteora was restful, and the life was simple and unpretentious.

Many of the writers associated with the *Century* flocked to Onteora, where such staid figures as William Cullen Bryant, Edmund C. Stedman, and James Russell Lowell could go picnicking in the woods and, in the evenings, lounge about the fire at the Bear and the Fox, the local inn where, as Candace Wheeler put it, "Mark Twain and Jamie Dodge—who surely had the gift—told stories, and Laurence Hutton and Brander Mathews contributed their share of the entertainment . . . while the . . . Gilders and some of our beloved painters smiled or laughed and listened."[26]

Dodge's cottage, Yarrow, was the center of a busy social life to which one witness reports, "gathered the most brilliant of the community": "Here wit and wisdom flashed and counterflashed, and in the midst of the brilliancy none was so brilliant, so scintillating, so humorous, so flashing as the beloved hostess herself. But so modest was she that she was never the chief actor. Instead she seemed to provide an atmosphere in which stories or other 'stunts'—always expected at these gatherings—became spontaneous and marvellously clever performances—a wonder at times to the producers themselves."[27] In the years from 1894 to 1905 Dodge took *St. Nicholas* as far as she could, but in the last years of this period she gradually withdrew from active management in favor of her associate, Fayal Clarke. Clarke carried on in Dodge's tradition and consulted with her frequently. Dodge encouraged the early work of artist-writers John Bennett and Howard Pyle and introduced the "Goops" of Gellett Burgess to her young readers. Lovers of adventure and excitement could read G. A. Henty and Jack London in *St. Nicholas*, as well as the old Rough Rider, Teddy Roosevelt. For Dodge herself as a writer, this was a period of consolidation and recycling of earlier work. *The Land of Pluck*,[28] a collection of stories, appeared in 1894, as did a book of verse, *When Life Is Young*.[29] In 1897 she published *A New Baby World*[30] and in 1898 both a compilation of material for performance called *The Children's Book of Recitations*[31] and a reissue—with major revisions—of her first book, *The Irvington Stories*.[32]

In July 1898 Fayal Clarke fell ill at Onteora and had to have an appendectomy. His recovery was slow, and when he was well enough to return to New York, he went into bachelor apartments not far from Dodge's flat. Agreeable, intelligent, hardworking, witty, and utterly reliable, Clarke had taken the place of Dodge's sons when they were gone. But devoted as he was to Dodge, Clarke came to feel—rightly enough—that he had given up the life of his own he might have had, and so decided, in 1899, to set up his own household. Dodge, who had exhausted herself nursing him, was ordered to Europe by her own doctor and by Frank Scott, then president of the Century Company, successor to Charles Scribner and Company as publisher of *St. Nicholas*. Dodge's aunt, Tillie Elder, spoke of the family's pride in Lizzie Dodge and of their sadness at the thought "of a powerful woman like Lizzie breaking down in health or spirits" (quoted Wright 1979, 208).

Dodge's symptoms seem to have been more than physical, and the trip abroad was a good idea. She visited Naples with her companion, Ida Medairy, and went on to Egypt. On their return to Italy, Dodge learned that her sister Sophie had died. Unable to return home in time for the funeral, the travelers continued to Florence, Rome, and Genoa, and sailed for New York in May 1899.

In 1899 Dodge made an editorial decision that would have far-reaching results. She hired the hardworking and conscientious Albert Bigelow Paine to run the St. Nicholas League, an organization that encouraged readers to study, work together and contribute stories, poems, artwork, and photographs to the magazine. There were many competitions in which contributors could win recognition for their work. The league trained and encouraged many young writers and artists who would one day become famous, among them Stephen Vincent Benét, Henry Steele Commager, Rachel Field, F. Scott Fitzgerald, Ring Lardner, Edna St. Vincent Millay, Eudora Welty, Edmund Wilson, and Elinor Wylie.

Dodge continued to make the most of her stockpile of old manuscripts, producing a number of new volumes largely of old material: she published *Rhymes and Jingles* in an enlarged edition[33] and another book, *Poems and Verses*,[34] about two-thirds of which had already seen the light of day in her earlier book *Along the Way*.

During these years Dodge depended more than ever on Fayal Clarke to manage the day-to-day running of *St. Nicholas*. Though after 1898 he no longer lived in her home, Clarke remained a frequent guest and visitor, and when in 1903—to the stunned amazement of all his friends—he announced his engagement, it was to Katharine Strickland, a young woman who was working for Dodge as nurse-companion. They both remained good friends with Dodge and were staying with her at Onteora when she died.

Advancing age and recurrent health problems made it natural enough for Dodge to withdraw gradually from active management of *St. Nicholas*. And the transition was made easier because, though the final editorial authority had always been hers, she had worked so closely with her staff that she had always been able to trust them "with the actual making of the magazine" (Clarke 1905, 1070). After a period of intermittent ill health, Dodge died at Onteora Park on 21 August 1905.[35]

The simple funeral service held at the Onteora church was concluded with a reading of Dodge's own poem "The Two Mysteries," and the following day a great cross of yarrow gathered by the children of Onteora was laid on her grave at the Evergreen Cemetery in Hillside, New Jersey. But as her friend and colleague Fayal Clarke said of her, "It is given to few to exercise so far-reaching an influence upon young minds, and thus upon the future of the nation. She left the world not only happier, but better than she found it" (Clarke 1905, 1071), and her best memorial is her lifework.

2

Early Journalism

To publicize his ideas about the role of science in the future of American agriculture, James Jay Mapes founded a periodical called, appropriately enough, the *Working Farmer*. Mapes's vivid personality and fluent, emphatic style gave his monthly magazine a distinctive editorial voice. A typical issue began with a long, earnest, and often-argumentative editorial piece on some favorite theme—the wonders worked by fertilizers, the merits of the Mapes subsoil plow, or the need to establish a Federal Department of Agriculture. Articles on plants, soils, farm machinery, crops, and news of interest to farmers usually followed. But Mapes also included articles of a general nature, designed to introduce his readers to the work of writers he admired. For example, he printed a piece by Herbert Spencer on child rearing, urging parents to read Spencer's *Education: Intellectual, Moral, and Physical* and "let its good seed blossom and fruit in the happy hereafter of your sons and daughters,"[1] and he presented some choice thoughts from Emerson on the importance of self-reliance for young men who wanted to succeed in life.[2]

Disseminating ideas and information from a wide variety of sources was a chief function of the journal. A department called "The Book Table" frequently offered summaries of the contents of the many magazines received by the editorial staff, including such prestigious British periodicals as the *Westminster Review, Black-*

wood's, and the *Edinburgh Review*. Articles pointed out as likely to be of interest to readers of Mapes's farm journal included pieces on such diverse topics as the infallibility of the Bible, slavery, alcohol, Dante and his English translators, church expansion and liturgical revision, ballads, the Kingdom of Italy, iron manufacture, and Motley's history of the Netherlands.[3]

Lizzie Dodge worked with her father, her brother Charley, and her father's young assistant Patrick "Pecky" Quinn on the *Working Farmer*. It is likely that she wrote a number of short unsigned pieces on a variety of subjects. A few articles are signed with the initials she used at this time, MED, like the recipe for kohlrabi, "a comparatively new acquaintance" that "should be at least treated civilly. . . . As it is generally cooked, one would be more apt to pronounce it a cross between the turnip and the paving stone, than to recognize its true character."[4] But many more articles sound like her work—for example, the letter supposedly from a housewife, "Mrs. E.D.K.," who isn't sure whether her garden's amazing fertility is owing to Professor Mapes's wonderful phosphate fertilizer or to the dishwater she has also been throwing on it.[5]

Working Farmer and United States Journal

To broaden the educative program of his magazine and appeal to a more varied class of readers, Mapes decided to expand the *Working Farmer*. In 1861 he purchased the *United States Journal*, and proposed to publish a new periodical, to be called the *Working Farmer and United States Journal*. He announced that though in the past he had devoted most of his *Working Farmer* to agricultural matters, his subscribers—he claimed 30,000—had called for a greater diversity of subject matter, including material that would be attractive to families. To meet this need, his "Miscellaneous Department" would be greatly expanded and the new periodical would be devoted to household affairs, literature, art, applied science, and current events. Mapes made his daughter Lizzie— who had written a great deal of "miscellaneous" material for the

Working Farmer—editor of the new and separate *United States Journal* section appended to each issue of the *Working Farmer*.

This was Dodge's first editorial responsibility, and the most striking thing about the first issue of the *United States Journal* is the confident tone in which the young editor spoke to her readers about the journal and what she hoped to make of it. Dodge's editorial persona was authoritative, yet friendly and approachable. She began by announcing to her readers that, "having been appointed Major Domo of this particular Department," she would like to comment on how she planned to run it. After promising to serve the interests of former readers of both journals, she added: "Those who expect this to be merely a 'Ladies' Corner,' will doubtless be disappointed, for we do not believe in fencing in a love story and a few recipes, etc., for the sole portion of one half of creation; but it will be something for all.—Revered spectacled eyes may peer out many a line in it worth finding, and Father, Mother, the boys and girls, down to the golden-haired, picture-loving wee one, will, we trust, find pleasure and profit in its columns."[6]

Dodge was determined to give her readers their due. Each subscriber, she felt, had a certain "right, title, and interest" in the contents of her paper, and she felt she would be a poor editor if she did not respect this prerogative: "We cannot stop here, after these fair assurances, without asking our readers to help us realize them. We shall do our best; but we want to *know* those for whom we write; we want to learn something of their tastes, their requirements, so that our best energies may be called forth, and no mis-directed labor expended. We ask them to write to us—to encourage, to find fault, if need be, and above all, to send good contributions for the benefit of each other" ("Readers," 256). Still, Dodge felt it necessary to make clear that as editor she would have the final say about what she would print, and warned that "there are two people . . . to whose counsel, should they chance to be subscribers, we cannot listen—they are my-lord Dogmatism and Mrs. Grundy, to whom not only our paper, but the 19th century itself, must continue to be 'out of joint' " ("Readers," 256).

Dodge's editorial work was carried on largely at home, where her whole family was often drawn into the project, and she adverts to this homey working style in her first editorial, using it as a guarantor of the wholesomeness and nurturing impulse characteristic of the whole enterprise: "In conclusion, we would say, that these pages are not concocted in a dusty down town office, with 'Our Paris Correspondent' writing in one corner, and 'Our Washington Correspondent' hard at work in another, but they are prepared within the precincts of a sunny *home*, and it is hoped that wherever they may go, they will carry a genuine home influence with them" ("Readers," 256). Many of the attitudes expressed in this opening editorial would prove to be characteristic of Dodge throughout her career: the humor, the determination not to be taken lightly because she was a woman, a fundamental confidence in herself, and her empathy and sense of responsibility toward her audience—including its youngest members.

A glance through the pages of this first of Dodge's editorial projects reveals many of the ideas that recur in her later work. A central theme in Dodge's writing is the importance of creative play to the development of children. And in the first issue of the new, family oriented *United States Journal* she gives prominent place to a discussion of the work of Friedrich Wilhelm Froebel:

> The "Kindergarten" or "Children's Garden," has long been established in Germany as a mode of education for young children. Its founder, Froebel, has already had followers in France and England, and, more recently, some philanthropists have attempted to introduce the system in the vicinity of Boston. It is based on the principle that, *the organization of childish play should be the first culture of the mind* and the method adopted is, to so encourage and systematize simple amusement, that the mind of the child is led into paths of beauty and order without constraining its activity ... [so that] at ten the child is ready to enter the severer school-life—with an earnest, opened nature, quickened observations, and a temper unsoured by the indiscriminate repression common to our usual school system.[7]

Dodge goes on to suggest that she is confident these new educational methods will become as popular as the many delightful Christmas customs imported from Germany, including "Chris-Cringle" and "the wealth and tenderness of the new 'Children's Literature,' which is fast twining itself in loving tendrils about the home life of America." There is much here to suggest the Dodge of *St. Nicholas*: the image of the children's pleasure garden as the ideal place to learn, the notion that "the organization of childish play should be the first culture of the mind," her conviction that it is better not to constrain the child's mind but to lead it gently, and her appreciation that there is a real need for variety and change in the pleasure offered the learning child ("Kindergarten," 258).

But Dodge also demonstrates some of the interesting practical concern she later showed for some children's intractable problems. She observes that until the schoolrooms of the very young can become happier and healthier places, perhaps it is better that children of this age should remain at home. The ideal would be for the home itself to become, as hers was, a true "kinder-garten." "Yet few homes," she says, "can have a 'kinder-garten' of their own—and there are besides, thousands of children of tender years, whose mothers are obliged to consign them to the care of others for a portion of each day." Just as her father used the editor's pulpit to preach reform of agriculture, Dodge used hers to speak out about changes she thought it necessary for Americans to make if their children were to become the kind of people who could shape a better future ("Kindergarten," 258).

Conventional errors of all kinds that tended to cramp and confine men and women were targets for Dodge's gentle but persistent criticism. She stressed the gradual progress women had made toward greater freedom, listing, for example, several of the notorious "blue laws" of Connecticut, some of which she said "will serve to remind us that the world has been pretty thoroughly ventilated since the days when the pilgrim fathers endured hardships innumerable, and the pilgrim mothers evinced an equal heroism, by enduring the pilgrim fathers."[8]

Reviewing a book called *Women's Right under the Law*, Dodge expressed her view that legislatures cannot be expected to "undo all the kinks in our great social chain, and to these, the best 'Women's Rights' demonstration of the day is the present glorious advance of our educational system." Yet she pays tribute to such earnest workers as the author of this book and wishes godspeed to "all efforts" "to make the race wiser and better."[9]

In a piece on "Pocket Money," on the same page, Dodge offered practical advice to husbands: "On the 1st of Jan., 1862, take the tightening gold and silver band from your wife's brain, and bid her think for herself. It may be a risk, especially for those who have married dolls instead of women—but every year most of you risk something in the hope of becoming rich—this time risk something in the hope of becoming happier."[10] In a number of other short pieces Dodge addressed girls, recommending healthy outdoor exercise (especially ice skating), "vigorously assisting in the employment of their elders," "enriching their minds," and avoiding idleness in favor of the sort of work they are best fitted for.[11] Dodge went out of her way to provide young girls with role models of active and accomplished women by featuring news items about famous women and by running a series of articles on famous heroines in American history who had fought beside men in battle, such as Molly Pitcher and Deborah Sampson.

Dodge herself was responsible for much of the material in her magazine but, like many editors before and since, liked to suggest that she had a large staff of writers, and so she frequently used pseudonyms. Her own copy of the complete run of her magazine in the Princeton University Library has penciled notations in her handwriting identifying many of the pieces as hers. Among the contents she chose to sign with pseudonyms were several mildly sensational stories. "Le Longue Carbine; or, The Borderer's Dream," by "Oununga," is a story told in the first person by an Indian who hates the destroyers of his people.[12] "Gaston Glencoe; an Incident in the Siege of Fort Meigs," by "Major Maxwell," tells of how a "borderer" named Glencoe outwits some Indians,[13] and "Mary Bennett" is a wish-fulfillment fantasy about the return of a husband, captured by Indians, after a five-year absence.[14]

Dodge's working notebooks for this period—if she kept any—

have not survived, but many of the occasional pieces in the *United States Journal* preserve for us Dodge's early attempts to play with an idea or device that she later expanded on in some better known work. Here are to be found a sober, factual article, "Shoddy,"[15] which may have provided the kernel for her later, more celebrated essay "Shoddy Aristocracy in America";[16] an article titled "The Rights of the Body,"[17] on which one of her later "Susan Snapp" pieces was built (*TO*, 236–39); and accounts of games and crafts projects that later appeared in *A Few Friends*.

Influence of Horace Scudder

In 1866 Horace Scudder asked Dodge to become a contributor to his new periodical for children, the *Riverside Magazine*. Scudder visited Dodge at Waverly, and the two editors found much common ground. Their letters reveal how closely they agreed on many basic issues and how warmly they supported each other with practical advice and assistance. Dodge believed in the importance of the sort of high-quality periodical for children that Scudder proposed and understood his concern that the magazine should be all it could be: "No wonder you feel 'solicitude' on some points. It is certainly a heavy responsibility as well as a high privilege to have the ear of young America once a month—but from the tone of your letter I feel sure it will hear only pure and genial and high-toned things from the new magazine. Something tells me that you are not starting it on an intensely literary basis, but that already it is a labor of love."[18]

Perhaps even more than Scudder, Dodge felt that children ought not to be preached at; the child audience deserved respect and attention. Again and again in her letters she speaks to Scudder of the importance of testing material on real child readers and taking their reactions seriously. She empathized with the feelings of a child audience that so often was at the mercy of adults who had forgotten what it is to be young: "The poor children! *We* have the privilege of hiring our preachers and selecting our own wise counsel—but they, poor things, are beridden with our preaching and counselling, and teaching, and often most dismal of all, amusing, from the hour of their toddlehood. It needs a merciful, wise, and a loving heart to deal with them—they are far more like ourselves than we think—but we often pour the lees of our experience upon them in a stream of twaddle expecting them to be edified and delighted while we smack our lips over the wine."[19]

Dodge's first piece for Scudder was a rambling, somewhat disjointed account of Dutch life called "The Funny Land of Pluck,"[20] quite probably based on notes she had taken for *Hans Brinker*. She apologized to Scudder for the way the material had seemed to expand as she worked on it, and said that since children "don't like baby talk upon grand subjects," she had tried to make her paper "suggestive and calculated to make young readers hungry for more information. . . . You can't squeeze such a wet sponge of a subject very much, you know, without making it dry, and that would never do for the Riverside."[21] Squeeze the subject she did, however, providing yet another installment, called simply "The Land of Pluck," in the September 1867 issue.[22] And she soon was ready to respond to another request from Scudder with a series of articles on toys and games. Dodge, who had always been interested in parlor games and who two years earlier had copyrighted a successful game called *The Protean Cards*, was well qualified to write the pieces.

"Holiday Whispers concerning Games and Toys," a brief survey of what was available in New York's toy stores, appeared just before Christmas in the January 1867 issue.[23] Though Dodge felt a little shy about singling out her own game for special praise, her business sense prevailed, and she compromised with her conscience by quoting the praise of a friend for the *Protean Cards*. In short succession there followed a series of pieces in which Dodge developed a form that would become something of a specialty: the amusing, smoothly written account of an entertaining set of party games or holiday festivities designed to serve readers as inspiration and resource for their own home entertainment. "Kaleidoscopes and Burglars,"[24] "Bessie's Birthday Party,"[25] "Croquet at Midnight,"[26] and "A Midnight Visit to Clio"[27] followed in due course.

Hearth and Home

In the spring of 1868 Dodge accepted a position as associate editor responsible for "Home and Miscellany" on a new weekly magazine called *Hearth and Home*, which would make its debut in December of that year. She would be working with coeditors Harriet Beecher Stowe and Donald G. Mitchell, who wrote under the name "Ik Marvel." The publishers were to be Pettingill, Bates, and Company, and Dodge's salary, as indicated in a letter to her from Robert Dale Owen, was to be $1,500 (Wright 1979, 54).

Dodge's work for *Hearth and Home* required her to commute by train and ferry from her home in Waverly, New Jersey, to the magazine's offices at 37 Park Row in New York City. Though Stowe was nominally Mitchell's coeditor, she did little of the practical, day-to-day editorial work, much of which fell to Dodge. In the first issue of *Hearth and Home* were contributions from Holmes and Trowbridge, as well as William Cullen Bryant's "Old World Sparrow." On the margin of the manuscript of this last piece, Dodge noted that "this poem was written for *me* (Mr. Bryant said) rather than for *Hearth and Home*" (quoted in Wright 1979, 54). Bryant had been close to James Jay Mapes, and so he was perhaps eager to please the daughter of an old friend. Dodge was already demonstrating that ability to persuade distinguished authors to write for her which marked her later career. She was always quick to capitalize on a social connection, and New York's literary and journalistic circles were for her sources of many important contacts.

Dodge's friend Horace Scudder served her well during this time. She asked his advice on technical matters—like the best way to make out a draft to pay her contributors—and he sent her a model draft on Hurd and Houghton and advised her to keep a contribution book, as he did. He also generously sent her a list of names and addresses of likely contributors and a list of the designers and wood engravers he preferred. Grateful to Scudder both for his practical help and for the opportunity to talk with him about larger issues and policies, Dodge wrote after one of his visits, "You helped me so very much when you were here that I feel like urging Messrs. P. and B to secure your services at $50,000 a year, as my mental & moral advisor."[28]

The children's department of *Hearth and Home* was described in advertising notices as "edited by Mrs. Mary Mapes Dodge, with many assistants,"[29] though in truth many of the names signed to individual contributions were Dodge pseudonyms, and much of the unattributed verse is hers, for it showed up later in her collection *Rhymes and Jingles*. To provide a friendly voice for the department, Dodge created the persona of "Uncle Tim," a rheumatic old gentleman with an evident affection for all his honorary nieces and nephews, whom Uncle Tim encouraged to participate actively in a dialogue with their favorite paper. He asked them teasing questions about natural history and offered prizes for solving puzzles called "Uncle Tim's Muddles." The last of these, "The Famous Fifteen Muddle," drew more than 11,000 responses.

Uncle Tim and his assistant, "The Little Schoolma'am"—a stickler for rules who turns up later in *St. Nicholas Magazine*—presided over a lively miscellany, including sentimental and didactic tales, translations, tidbits of information on famous people, how-to hints, games, puzzles, charades, anagrams, and verse. Under Dodge's care the journal's children's pages became quite a success. Dodge, always a good businesswoman, was coming to appreciate her own worth. On 27 September 1869 she wrote to James H. Bates, one of the publishers of *Hearth and Home*, that though she felt the work she did for them "congenial," she could not afford to continue to work for "a salary less than from $2000 to $2500." She also noted that her engagement to them would expire in November, and made it quite clear that they would have to pay her price or lose her services.[30]

Pettingill and Bates raised her salary, even though their enterprise was not on sound financial footing. By the following year, 1870, they sold *Hearth and Home* to the Orange Judd Company. The new proprietors replaced Mitchell (Stowe had left the previous year) and raised Dodge's salary to $3,000. But she was working harder than ever and was now sorely in need of help. It was at this time that Dodge hired Frank Stockton, a young Philadelphian whose work she had come to admire in the *Riverside Magazine* as

well as in *Hearth and Home.* In later years Stockton was fond of
telling the story of his first meeting with Dodge: "From the fact
that she was 'a writer and editor for little folks,' [Stockton] had
conceived an ideal of her as 'a tall, spare, angular woman, very
old-maidish in appearance, with a Maria Edgeworth type of face,
spectacles at her eyes, and little round curls dangling in front of
her ears.' When, therefore, on entering her sanctum in the office
of 'Hearth and Home,' he was greeted warmly . . . by 'one of the
most attractive and brilliant women he had ever seen,' aglow
with enthusiasm and wit, he was surprised almost to the point of
embarrassment" (Clarke 1905, 1068). The journal's circulation
increased, and Dodge's departments became a more prominent
part of the weekly issues. Soon her reputation as a clever editor
"equaled that which she had already attained as author." Fayal
Clarke related an incident connected with her work on *Hearth
and Home* that suggests why she was so successful:

> A happy idea came to her that would, she knew, greatly
> improve the number of the paper just then going to press.
> But—it involved a change of many pages, the rewriting
> of almost the entire contents of her department, and—
> the presses were waiting. A consultation was quickly
> held; the project was outlined and was promptly declared
> by all to be an inspiration. But could it be carried out in
> time? A half-hour went by in discussion; and then the
> decision was gently broken to Mrs. Dodge in the words:
> "It is impossible. We are very sorry but it is impossible."
>   "Yes, I know. It *is* impossible, of course. But let's do it,
> just the same! Why not?" was the quick, inspiring reply;
> and it was done—to the final enthusiastic admiration of
> all concerned. (Clarke 1905, 1064)

But Dodge never had had a completely free hand in her work for
Hearth and Home, and when a better opportunity appeared she
was, as she confided to her sister Kate, "delighted to be through
with H and H."[31]

Journalism for an Adult Audience

Though Dodge is best known for her writing and editing for children, she also did writing for adults. Much of this writing was in the form of occasional essays, easily written and easily forgotten. But Dodge herself cared enough about some of them to wish to preserve them in a collection of her pieces for adults called *Theophilus and Others*, and these deserve critical attention.

When, in the late 1870s, J. Blair Scribner told Dodge that his firm "wanted to do *any* book of hers" and would feel hurt if she were ever to turn to another publisher, Dodge collected a group of stories and essays that had already been published and offered them to him (Wright 1979, 94). Dodge was proud of the pieces in this collection and hoped it would do well with the public. When Edward Seymour of Scribner's asked her for help in getting together the advertising for the book, Dodge offered him a few "hints," though she described herself as laboring "under the difficulties of a strange combination of great modesty and intense conceit" in doing so.[32]

Dodge's advertising stratagems included stressing the international reputation she had acquired and centering on the humor of the pieces: "Will you allow me to blushingly suggest that the criticism generally made of the various sketches in this collection is that they possess the quality of humor, and many of the old notices spoke of the immortal Mrs. D., as, distinctively, that very rare thing—a female humorist."[33]

When *Theophilus and Others* was published by Scribner, Armstrong in 1876, one reviewer commented on the gentle naturalness of Dodge's humor, with its "jets of gleaming fun" and "veins of pathos." Looking at "everyday's concerns with honest and kindly eyes, as well as with a keen sense of the humorous," Dodge was said to make "the reader think well of all mankind, despite its follies."[34] The collection includes three engaging stories of the ups and downs in the life of a young married couple, two topical essays, a series of sketches, and a set of comic pieces.

The Theophilus Stories

The first three stories in the book are "Theophilus" stories, humorous accounts of domestic life in New York City during the Civil War. The stories are told in the first person by Em, who is married to a rising young businessman named Theophilus Brown. Theophilus is dignified and proper, and would like to cut a good figure in society; however, life seems to defeat him at every turn. In the first story, "Dobbs's Horse," he must make do with servants who are rough diamonds, a country house smaller and less improved than he would wish, and a horse that looks elegant but bolts when startled.

"Philly and the Rest" is really a discussion of the tendency of parents to lavish on their children a kind of "weak, doting admiration" (*TO*, 57) that robs them of their innocence and makes them self-conscious. Dodge comes out in favor of letting children enjoy their childhoods and warns parents that "all precocious development is hurtful: premature ability, premature politeness, premature pleasures, premature goodness even" (*TO*, 59).

In "Our Aggy" Em has taken into her home a young black girl, Aggy, who has escaped from slavery in the South. Theophilus, the "ease loving propriety-worshipping master of the house" (*TO*, 66), has been persuaded to let Em try to train the girl as a servant. Em, who is dominated by Theophilus in many ways, notes but does not seem to understand the way Theophilus's bossiness brings out an impish disobedience in Aggy. The piece ends in a reflective, bittersweet mood. While Aggy is walking Em's baby in its pram, softly singing it a freedom song, Theophilus roars an order at her from the window, and she bolts with the baby. After a comic chase scene, the baby is returned but Aggy has slipped away forever. Em never quite understands or admits all she has in common with Aggy. The ending of the story is tinged with regret: Em has failed to reach the girl, but she knows she will never forget her.

Again and again in these stories, Theophilus and Em have the wind taken out of their sails as nature—or human nature—proves more complex and intractable than they have supposed. Although Theophilus imagines he always knows best and Em prides herself on knowing how to manage him, things rarely turn out as either of them expects.

"Shoddy"

"Shoddy Aristocracy in America," reprinted as "Shoddy" in *Theophilus and Others*, deals with the phenomenon of "new money." Dodge comments on the deplorable taste of the newly rich after the Civil War and offers some Dickensian sketches from life, but she also notes that the education of whole new classes will open new opportunities for the poor and will promote national prosperity. Because the article was based on personal observation and contained outspoken criticism of American society, it was sent to the *Cornhill Magazine* in England "as a publication safely removed from the comedy and the actors it presented." To Dodge's surprise and pleasure, "by return post she received a draft for £50 and a request from the *Cornhill* for a series of papers."[35] But the biggest surprise of all was the great interest taken in the piece by the American press, which reprinted it widely, often without attribution.

"Insanity of Cain"

The second of Dodge's essays to gain broad acclaim was her amusing "Insanity of Cain," written in 1872. Though Dodge elsewhere[36] is sympathetic to the view that circumstances may diminish criminal responsibility, she here satirizes the idea. After examining the peculiar strains of his upbringing and natural endowment, "hereditary organism, temperamental excitability, emotional phrensy" (*TO*, 103), Dodge suggests that the reasonable verdict on Adam's firstborn would surely be not guilty by reason of insanity—"our children and our children's children must be taught to speak of Cain the manslaughterer; Cain the mentally excitable; Cain the peculiarly circumstanced; but Cain the Murderer? Never!" (*TO*, 103). Having made her case, Dodge leaves the question to the "intelligence and the justice of this faithful and enlightened century" (*TO*, 104).

This article was said to have arisen "out of a remark to Mr. Roswell Smith when Mrs. Dodge and he were discussing the re-

cent acquittal of a criminal on the plea of emotional insanity."
Dodge quipped that "they will be saying next that Cain was in-
sane," and Smith reportedly asked her to write an article on the
subject, the piece eventually appearing in *Scribner's Monthly* in
May 1873 (Tutwiler, 261). The truth of the matter may be a little
different. The basic idea of a comically straight-faced defense of
Cain as an innocent victim of circumstance is perhaps derived
from an essay in a book written by Dodge's grandfather, Garrit
Furman, a copy of which is among Dodge's papers at Princeton.[37]

The article was well received by critics. Though a religious
newspaper took Dodge to task "for what the critic regarded a
sentimental but serious defense of crime," the more perceptive
Scribner's Monthly described it as "a satire so deftly managed
that it shines with real fun, while it cuts deep into the thoughts
and motives of men."[38]

Sketches and Comic Pieces

"My Mysterious Enemy," a story first published in *Harper's*, is
a long-drawn-out joke on the reader. In the manner of Edgar Allan
Poe it recounts the way an innocent young woman staying in a
New York boardinghouse is stalked by another inmate of the
house, and attacked while sleeping in her own bed. The story
reaches what appears to be a lurid climax when the victim describes how "with the strength of a maniac" (*TO*, 155) she beat her
tormentor to death with a bedpost. The joke is that the mysterious
enemy in question is, of course, a rat, not a human being, and
Dodge teasingly suggests that if "the reader of this narrative" has
"taken the slaughtered rat 'for his better,' . . . he has read with
his imagination instead of his eyes: 'a bad habit; I pray you to
avoid it' " (*TO*, 157).

In 1870, when Richard Watson Gilder was editing *Scribner's
Monthly*, one of his contributors let him down at the last minute,
and he appealed to Dodge for a piece of "filler." Dodge gave in to
the request and described what then happened this way:

> "With not an idea in my head, I sat for a while gazing
> vacantly into space, and then, perhaps because there was

no possible connection between the task in hand and a quick-witted Irish cook we had, she flashed before my mental vision and persistently filled it, obscuring everything except the blank sheet and a miserable consciousness of Mr. Gilder waiting confidingly downstairs. What key of association brought to mind the name of a Chinese servant of my sister, in San Francisco, is equally inexplicable—but in the imaginary by-play between these two characters the article took shape. The only difficulty was to write fast enough. When, an hour or so later, I carried it down to Mr. Gilder he tried to look pleased, but I have always felt that in time he must have shared my surprise at the public appreciation which it received." (Tutwiler, 262)

"Miss Malony on the Chinese Question" was much admired, and the story of its writing gained Dodge a reputation for being able to respond quickly and produce high-quality work on demand. The piece is essentially a dramatic monologue in which an Irish cook describes to a friend her outrage at being expected to work with a new Chinese servant her mistress has just hired. Fing Wing copes with a world in which so much is new and strange to him by copying everything Miss Malony does, from taking off his shoes when he peels potatoes to stealing groceries and putting them in Miss Malony's secret hiding place. Dodge's portrayal of the immigrant servants here reflects the casual racism and ethnic bias of her class and time. But she handles the Irish accent cleverly, and her presentation of the prejudice of one immigrant toward another gives the piece an interesting edge. The sketch was a popular performance piece and was frequently done on stage by the celebrated Charlotte Cushman, who liked it so well that she asked Dodge for more Irish sketches (Wright 1979, 82).

In her letters Dodge sometimes prefaces a mildly outrageous quip with "as Susan Snapp might say." The persona of Snapp, a clever, sophisticated woman with a wry sense of humor, gave Dodge license to be a bit flippant and impertinent. The "Little Talks" by Susan Snapp included in the collection are short, lively

monologues on women drivers, boring house guests, shrewd coun-
tryfolk, and inconsiderate husbands.

Dodge said that "What a Little Song Can Do: A True Incident"
was based on an actual event in her life. The story is a simple
one, about a dressmaker whose life has been a series of disasters
but who manages to keep going by taking one day at a time. Her
formula for survival is contained in a set of verses by Adelaide
Procter called "One by One" that the dressmaker keeps in her
workbasket. The story is no more memorable than the verses, but
the narrator's initial confession to the reader that servants and
other "employees of all kinds" "hold a mysterious power" over her
based on the guilt they make her feel is interesting in light of the
thematics of some of the other pieces in the collection. She says
"I shrink from my waiter-girl, and feel condemned in the presence
of my cook." She is almost tempted to tell them that it is not
entirely her fault "that some must work while others play" (*TO*,
160).

"The Spirit of the Waterfall" is a dream-vision in which Ella
M'Flimsey is shown the error of her ways by a goblinlike creature.
Ella is a frivolous, vain, fashionable woman, with a roomful of
unread books and undone tasks, a woman who never seriously
gives an opinion or utters a sentiment that might truly reveal
the kind of person she is. She is beautiful, but her fiancé senses
something false and deceptive about her loveliness. One night
after a reception she returns to her room, and there the goblin
summons up the spirits of the many women and girls whose hair
had been cut off to make the false curls, braids, and "fall" Ella
had worn to dazzle her admirers.

The true owners of the hair turn out to be women whose lot in
life is very different from Ella's—a mother who had to sell her
starving baby's curls, a lunatic whose hair was cut off in the
madhouse, a convict whose hair was stolen from her before she
was executed, and numberless other dim, careworn figures. The
intense guilt evoked in this story at the wearing of false hair is
perhaps understandable if Ella is seen here as a representative
of a society that has brutally and thoughtlessly taken from these
unfortunates the last thing of value they possessed. It is signifi-

cant that Ella's honesty at the end of the story is accompanied by a new thoughtfulness that also charms her admirers.

"Sunday Afternoon in a Poorhouse" describes a visit by the narrator and her friend to one of New York's houses of refuge. The narrator's companion talks to the overseer and comes away "filled with grand philanthropic ideas" (*TO*, 192), while the narrator, who has spent her time with the inmates, is troubled by images of what she has seen there and filled with "a choking sense of human misery" (*TO*, 193).

Though Dodge apparently thought well of the stories and sketches in *Theophilus and Others*, their interest to modern readers is limited. Some are graceful, amusing pictures of middle-class domestic life of the period; others are interesting because their popularity tells us something about the tastes of the time; and still others manage to express, while ostensibly dealing with happy middle-class life, the deep-seated guilt of the prosperous in a society in which it was all too easy to come to financial grief. Over and over again in these pieces the good things in life are seen to be held by a few who may have done nothing to deserve them and might lose them at any moment. Dodge's essays and sketches were valued for their graceful style and lively humor; underneath the polished surface, however, a strain of anxious uneasiness adds a dark note to many of them.

3

The Irvington Stories

The Irvington Stories, based in part on stories Dodge had told her own sons, appeared in 1865. Though it was not a best-seller, the collection went through several editions quickly enough to establish publisher James O'Kane's confidence in Dodge's ability to appeal to her chosen audience. Dodge's good friend Lu Runkle observed that "the stories had just enough of improbability to suit the minds of children, for whom the age of fancy and fable renews itself in every generation," while the strong moral undertone appealed to their parents (Runkle, 285). The *Working Farmer*, reflecting the views of those closest to Dodge, commented on Dodge's respect for her young readers: "These stories are not written in the 'Harry and Lucy' style, but appeal to the appreciation of children by tacitly recognizing them as on the same plane as the writer. No child likes to be patted on the head while he is reading, but imbibes instruction far more readily if his capacity to comprehend the subject is taken for granted. The Irvington Stories aim to please and to invigorate—to teach without stating what is *taught*, and thus convey instruction, improve the moral tone, and inculcate proper principles in the most effectual way."[1]

The warm and reassuring maternal persona that informs the narrative voice of *The Irvington Stories* explicitly supports traditional values parents might see as likely to help their children hold a steady course in a time of great social change and moral

42

confusion: hard work, obedience, religious reverence, patriotism, duty. Yet the best of the stories Dodge told also expressed on a symbolic level many of the unspoken feelings and needs of her child readers.

The Irvington Stories went through four early editions with O'Kane. Thirty-three years later, H. L. Allison, son of an old friend and co-worker of James Jay Mapes, approached Dodge—now a well-established figure in the literary world—with the idea of issuing another edition. Dodge dropped some of the weaker stories and added five more pieces and a preface explaining to a new generation of young readers that the stories had been written long ago and that she had, as the years went by, written "other books that seemed to her better suited to the changing times" but had decided to issue this edition so that it could be enjoyed by the children of her original readers (quoted in Wright 1979, 206).

The ten items in the 1864 edition of the collection are extremely varied. Dodge uses a number of voices and styles, and attempts different genres. The group includes two didactic poems, a fable in the Hans Christian Andersen mode, a biographical anecdote, a tall tale, a patriotic song, and four ambitious short stories: a weird, *Struwwelpeter*-like dream-vision; a sentimental Christmas story; a timely bit of fiction about the Civil War; and a violent tale about children kidnapped by Indians. In her 1898 revision Dodge dropped the biographical anecdote and the tall tale and added three moral tales and two accounts of family festivities.

Several of the shorter pieces in *The Irvington Stories* are literary experiments, less interesting for their intrinsic merit than for what they can tell us about Dodge's effort to master the craft of writing for children. "The Golden Gate" is a fable in the Andersen tradition about a poor child who heeds the Gospel admonition to "love thy neighbor" and a rich one, who doesn't. Three of the stories in the revised 1898 version might also be described as moral fables of one sort or another: "Dick and the Bantams," "All in a Day," and "Learning by Heart."

"The Artist and the Newsboy," the biographical anecdote included in the original edition, concerns the painter Inman, whose picturesquely ragged newsboy model tries to make himself more presentable by washing himself and getting his hair cut. In doing so, he loses the very charm that has made him appealing to the artist. The newsboy is seen from an adult's point of view, and the artist's desire to exploit his colorful raggedness is presented sympathetically. The boy is perceived as an aesthetic object rather than a person, and is considered foolish for having chosen to alter his appearance according to his own taste and, presumably, that of his social class. Dodge's treatment of the newsboy is mawkish, and the story is likely to seem sentimental and patronizing to modern tastes. The author here may be writing about a child, but she is not speaking effectively to a child audience. Dodge herself probably sensed that this was not her best work, for it is one of those she dropped in the revised edition, along with an even weaker sketch called "Brave Robbie and the Skeleton."

Two of the pieces added to the 1898 edition are slight accounts of family festivities. One, "The Wonderful Well: A Christmas Sketch from Life," is a reminiscence of one of Dodge's own dazzling childhood Christmases at her Grandmother Mapes's house in New York, a party attended by Lizzie, Louise, Sophie, and all the cousins and relations. The event is recalled through a child's eyes, and the mystifications of a family Christmas surprise are presented so that observant young readers can guess for themselves how Lizzie's cousins made a magic well, a fairy, and an outsize monkey appear in the grandmother's back parlor. This evocation of a warm family celebration with lots of games and an elaborate gift-giving ritual explores a situation that appears frequently in Dodge's fiction. Here, the party games and music are described so carefully as to make the piece almost a how-to article.

Another, similar description, "A Doll's Party: A Sketch from Real Life," presents a picture of a party for girls "under eleven," but the event sounds more appropriate for quite young children. What point the piece has in the telling seems to come from the narrator's choosing to treat the little girls as the "mothers" of their dolls, and the children's social event appears to be a solemn imitation of an elaborate adult party with a good deal of conspicuous consumption. The appeal to children might be like the appeal of an animated Christmas window in a fashionable toy store:

everything is miniature, pretty, elaborate, expensive—fascinating to look at, if a little out of reach of the average child.

Dodge's more ambitious pieces, "The Hermit of the Hills," "Cushamee; or, The Boy's Walk," "Po-No-Kah: An Indian Tale," and "Captain George, the Drummer-Boy: A Story of the Rebellion," offer variations on themes and story patterns that were to preoccupy her throughout her career. Among them are three basic formulas that R. Gordon Kelly identifies as prominent in the sort of fiction that was later to appear in *St. Nicholas*: the "ordeal," the "change of heart," and the "gentry mission" (Kelly 1974, 38).

The ordeal involves isolation; the need to respond quickly and decisively to some challenge, trial, or temptation; and the return to the adult world of the family, where there will be a reward for the performance. Kelly compares the pattern with Arnold Van Gennep's rite-of-passage paradigm involving separation, isolation, and transition and incorporation into a new social world or reintegration with an older world. This pattern is especially clear in a story like "Capt. George."

The change-of-heart formula often follows a similar basic plot pattern but involves the protagonist's conversion, "a dramatic shift in perception which combines a conscious recognition of the erroneous nature of the individual's former behavior with a conscious resolution to do better" (Kelly 1974, 43). Although a number of change-of-heart stories are found in *The Irvington Stories*, probably the most striking is the story of Tom Laffer, in "Cushamee," who learns not to torment dumb animals or tease his little sister.

The gentry mission involves a "figure who embodies the moral values of gentility and whose moral force brings about a change in the values of others" (Kelly 1974, 47–48). (It is not unusual for such values to be carried forward by a very young person.) Dodge's drummer boy, George, teaches a young comrade how to write and opens up a new world to him; the kindness of young Elsie to the unsociable old hermit she befriends in "The Hermit of the Hills" restores him to his family, to his community, and to an active social role in bringing happiness to the children of the town.

In Dodge's practice, the ordeal, the change of heart, and the gentry mission are often incorporated in a story pattern that might be termed Dodge's own personal myth of the fractured family. Over and over in her stories, families are parted by some sudden disaster (accident, shipwreck, war, kidnapping) and can be reunited only through the generosity and faithfulness of some member of the group who effects a healing. Frequently, though not always, the initial rupture of the family unit occurs because a father figure refuses—or is unable—to play his traditional role as guardian, guide, and protector. The story then dramatizes what the father's failure means to the family: a painful separation, followed by some providential intervention and the coming together of the group again—healed and whole.

"The Hermit of the Hills" and "Cushamee"

"The Hermit of the Hills" is a sentimental Christmas story in which a child's kindness restores an old man to the family he had long ago rejected. The hermit, a seemingly stern, cold, and lonely man, had cut himself off from his daughter when she married against his wishes. A little girl—who turns out to be his granddaughter—offers him an act of kindness, and he is transformed into a benevolent figure who gives a Christmas party for the children of the town and is reunited with his family.

When she wrote this story, Dodge still had much to learn about writing effectively for children. The story has a dull beginning and a gushy tone: the young protagonist is termed a "tender-hearted creature" (*IS*, 18), "a noble-hearted child" (*IS*, 19), and "our little Samaritan" (*IS*, 18). The strengths of the piece lie in Dodge's careful observation of the way children behave at play and in her elaboration of the particulars of a Christmas celebration.

In "Cushamee; or, The Boy's Walk" Dodge offers a didactic fable structured like a dream-vision in which a demonic figure takes the protagonist on an instructive journey. Here Tom Laffer refuses to play "Pap-pa" to his sister's doll and scornfully announces that if he were king, he'd "cut off the head of every doll in the land; or else . . . hang all the girls" (*IS*, 59). Tom has habitually treated helpless animals with similar brutality, but when girls and dolls feel his wrath, the story suggests he has gone too far. Retribution comes as he is summoned from sleep by the demonically animated figure of his sister's doll, Cushamee. Cushamee's voice has a strange authority, and she exercises absolute power over him. The doll is a rigid, robotlike figure whose feet rattle, jerk, and click along—a wonderful effect (rather like the "New Mother" of Mrs. Clifford, with her flashing lights and wooden tail). Tom is brought to book for his sins against frogs, cats, birds, and ants by being tormented by each in turn. Each time he is compelled to beg for mercy, and each time he hears a pitiless refrain from his former victims, denying that he has any right to clemency. The cats, for example, say, "how can an animal who can't see in the dark, and never eats mice, have any feeling?" (*IS*, 63), thus echoing the kind of sentiment with which Tom has justified his own brutality toward them. The story is very much in the tradition of didactic tales warning young boys not to be cruel to animals, yet it is especially interesting in its extension of that lesson to include scornful treatment of little girls and refusal to enter into their family-oriented doll play. After a final moment of hallucination in which Cushamee seems to swell to enormous proportions as her wooden arms shake him and a dreadful roll call of his misdeeds is intoned, Tom wakes up, chastened and repentant.

"Captain George, the Drummer-Boy"

"Captain George, the Drummer-Boy: A Story of the Rebellion" is Dodge's answer to her father's request that she write a story for boys about the Civil War. Dodge herself felt that "George" was the best piece in *The Irvington* Stories and was pleased when General McClellan, after reading it in manuscript form, told her it was "the finest and most accurate war story for boys that he had seen."[2] The young protagonist's father has died during the war, and at 14, much to his widowed mother's regret, he enlists in the Union Army as a drummer boy. He finds soon enough that the reality of a soldier's life is very different from that depicted in the war stories he has read in books. George becomes a hero,

but the warm family reunion that ends the story is somewhat
shadowed by Dodge's realistic depiction of the war's real cost in
human suffering.

While "Capt. George" appears on one level to be a straightforward response to James Mapes's suggestion that his daughter
write a patriotic tale for boys interested in the war then raging
between the states, the story she creates is more complex than its
formulaic nature might suggest. The inner life of the child with
whom young readers are asked to identify is honestly presented
as full of contradictions, incoherences, and dilemmas that cannot
be resolved. The protagonist's guilt and confusion are not directly
commented on in the narration, but they are vividly dramatized.

"Capt. George" combines elements of the ordeal and the gentry
mission with Dodge's favorite plot of the family reunited after
separation. Although the Bensons place a high value on patriotism, they are also committed to learning and to religious values.
The contradictory demands of religion and patriotism on the individual in time of war are symbolized in the story by George's
agonized conflict over his allegiance to the Bible and to the flag.
The story dramatizes George's frustrated effort to understand
and communicate his experience to a world that prefers patriotic
clichés to the truth.

Over and over, George insists in letters to his mother, sister,
and little brother that the war to which he has come is not the
one he has known from stories. The narrator comments: "To city
displays and story books, he soon discovered, belonged the glitter-
ing show he had expected to see—the great, regular masses of
men, line after line, marching close, with colors flying, music
sounding, and grand displays of cavalry and dazzling cannon,
adding their charm to the scene" (IS, 88). The reality was "not
picture soldiers" but "jaded, weary men, dust-soiled and nearly
dust-choked—though they marched on sturdily enough" under
"not picture-banners" but "war-stained, tattered flags" (IS, 89).

Though an excellent correspondent, George frequently finds
himself unable to tell his mother and sister directly about the
details of camp life. Dodge translates the brutalizing effect of
battle on young men into terms her readers can understand by

having George reflect on his fellow soldiers' cruelty to animals. He describes how the men kill rabbits with stones in the tense moments before battle, and adds in a letter to his sister, "This may seem very cruel to you—and I suppose it is so—but a soldier's time often hangs heavy on his hands. I would not like to trust your wonderful white kitten before the troops, even five minutes before a battle. They would certainly make a rush at it—every man of them" (*IS*, 102).

In one incident George is given important military dispatches to carry but is captured by rebel guerillas who force him to prove his cover story (that he's run away from the Union Army) by making him give a cheer for Jefferson Davis. George's anxiety and guilt over even a nominal betrayal of his ideals is made painfully clear as he chokes out a reluctant cheer for the rebel cause in the interest of protecting the important dispatches he is carrying. When the rebels go a step further and ask him to kiss the Bible for Jefferson Davis, George is faced with a more serious dilemma. If he fails to do so and is killed, as the guerillas threaten, the dispatches will certainly not go through, and they may fall into the rebels' hands. If he does as they say, he commits perjury and, in his own eyes, a kind of blasphemy. His duty to his country can justify a simple lie, but not this. He shouts, "Never!" and suddenly spurs his horse forward to escape (*IS*, 114). George is shot and falls from his horse, but the rebels erroneously assume he's been killed and leave him for dead without searching his body.

George manages to make his way back to camp, where he is hailed as a hero. But the incident has brought forward subtle issues of loyalty and honor that are not really resolved by the convenient error of the rebels. And though George is treated as a hero throughout the latter part of the story—treated as if what he's done has been planned and disciplined military action instead of the happy result of the guerillas' carelessness—it is clear that the whole experience has left him feeling, at some level, uneasy and guilty.

When George's general gives him the $1,000 his officers have collected as a farewell gift for their heroic drummer boy, George, knowing that his religious scruples have led him to endanger his comrades, tells the general he doesn't deserve the gift. The general, quoting Shakespeare, suggests that complete purity of motive and action are perhaps not possible for human beings: "Use every man after his desert, / And who shall scape whipping?" (*IS*, 139).

The story is full of patriotic rhetoric, yet when George leaves his home for the army, the reader is told that anyone "expecting to see a fiery youth waving an American flag over his head, . . . would have seen only a small boy sobbing in the arms of a mild-faced little woman" (*IS*, 76). Against the patriotic certitudes that might have been expected to dominate a war story for young children Dodge has posed the domestic values cultivated in the (mother-oriented) Benson home: reverence toward God, honesty, kindness, civility.

Tested by a series of father figures, George does his best to respond to their sometimes contradictory and often impossible requests. His father's last words propel him into a world where complex orders must be relayed in the simple code of the drum calls he is taught, a world that coarsens and can make cruel the people in it—can make demands on them beyond their capacity, perhaps against their personal ethical code. His captain's request that he carry the dispatches catapults George into the hands of the guerillas and an impossible dilemma. The general gives him money and a prize that he feels he does not deserve and then implicitly tells George that in the real world of war—as opposed to the storybook world—there can be no heroes.

In "Capt. George" Dodge has successfully adapted the formulas of popular fiction to express a more complex and nuanced view of the problematic moral relationship between children and their elders than is often found in children's fiction. A parent giving "Capt. George" a cursory reading might be led to believe that the story would affirm both the family values reflected in George's promises to his mother (that while away with the army he will never do anything to make her blush) and his commitment to carry out his father's intention to do his best to save the Union. A child reader inclined to identify more clearly with George would be likely to empathize with the frustration and uncertainty

George suffers while trying to do justice to incompatible ideals at the behest of rival authorities.

There was apparently some concern about including this story—which had been well received when it was first written—in the later 1898 edition. The fear was that it might arouse old prejudices and local animosities. Dodge, however, decided to include the story with the following comments:

> To the boys and girls of to-day, our Civil War seems almost like Ancient History. Well, even to their fathers and mothers it all seems to have happened very long ago. For the changing times have become changed indeed—changed and settled. Our country has passed through another war, and in its hours of trial and triumph the once divided nation has become more than ever molded into one. The foes of that day are comrades now. They have fought side by side in a common cause, and to-day there is no North, no South, but a re-united, glorious country. And no one rejoices over this more than Captain George—he, too, a grown man now. And his home is in the sunny South. (Quoted in Wright 1979, 206)

"Po-no-kah"

"Po-no-kah: An Indian Tale" is modeled to some extent on a popular literary form, the Indian captivity narrative. Beginning in the seventeenth century, tales of settlers' experiences at the hands of Indian captors in the wilderness were widely read by children as well as adults. The early narratives were cast in an allegorical mode and thematically showed young people "the horrors of captivity in Biblical terms that reaffirmed their dependence upon a parental God. Both captives and readers were, after all, the children of Israel; and the slaughters of innocent children were vividly portrayed."[3] But the narratives also satisfied their young readers' taste for "excitement, suspense, and terror" (Mendlicott, 25).

During the nineteenth century, captivity stories gradually became less like religious tracts and more like romantic adventure fiction. Dodge's Indians are seen by the adult settlers in her story as demonic savages, but on closer inspection the children find many qualities in them to admire. Though Dodge expresses disapproval of the violence the children must endure, she makes it clear that their encounter with an alternative culture enriches their lives in surprising ways.

The story begins with an evocation of the difference between the safe, comfortable, upper-middle-class home of the implied readers and the narrator (complete with references to napkin rings and silver saltcellars) and the precarious life of the frontier settler, who "after cheerfully leaving home in the morning for a day's hunt" would "return at night to find his family murdered or captured, and his cabin a mass of smoking ruins" (*IS*, 160). Although it relies on stereotyped characterization and formulaic action, the story depicts quite frankly the subversive appeal of both the wilderness and Indian life to its young protagonists.

While exploring the forest, Rudolph Hedden, five, and his sister, Kitty, three, are captured and brought to an Indian camp, where they face many dangers. Fortunately for them, they fall under the protection of a powerful old Indian woman named Ka-te-qua—a strong, independent mother figure who is fierce, yet nurturing. The wisdom and eloquence with which old Ka-te-qua is allowed to describe her way of raising children offers a real challenge to the settlers' values, and might well leave young readers poised between rival views of the central situation. In a sense the story follows a familiar Dodge scenario in which family life is destroyed by a father's mistake and, after a period of suffering involving many ordeals and tests, the family is reunited through the courage and endurance of the younger generation.

In "Po-no-kah," however, an almost-forgotten good deed done to an Indian by Farmer Hedden also proves vital to the happy ending. At the story's conclusion, Po-no-kah, a brave who has been fed and sheltered by Mr. Hedden, leads the children and their companion, Tom, back to their home, where he gives thanks in a speech echoing the New Testament: "Po-no-kah was cold and hungry; the father of the young pale-faces gave him food" (*IS*, 235). The kind brave strides majestically away, and the final section of the story stresses the message that a good deed is never forgotten. When *The Irvington Stories* was reissued in 1898, Dodge expressed a concern in her preface to the collection that the picture of Indian life presented in this story might give a distorted view of it to her readers, to whom "the tale of 'Po-no-kah' will be tempered by what they may have read or heard of the present condition of tribes of American Indians, who with the help of noble workers in their behalf, have made good progress towards civilization and education." She added, "Po-no-kah is but one example out of many, showing how certain men of his race have been distinguished by high traits of character even under the most savage conditions" (quoted in Wright 1979, 206).

Although the parents who purchased *The Irvington Stories* might well have been attracted by the educational program presented in the didactic verses that frame the volume, the children who read and loved the stories in the book were presented with a much more mixed—and more interesting—message. Dodge saw these children as responsible moral agents with the future in their hands, and since "The heritage of noble work / Descends from sire to son" (*IS*, 256), she urged on them the virtues she felt they needed: courage, truth, honor, learning, civility, loyalty, and generosity. But she also peopled her stories with very human boys and girls and set them in a complex world where choices are difficult and being good is not easy. This honesty to children's experience may explain something of Dodge's ability to engage the sympathy of younger readers as well as the confidence of their parents.

4

Hans Brinker

For most readers, it is *Hans Brinker; or, The Silver Skates* for which Mary Mapes Dodge is remembered today.[1] The title brings to mind quaint Dutch backgrounds, a fresh holiday atmosphere, skating races on the canal, the appealing boy and girl protagonists, and the unforgettable story of the little boy with his finger in the dyke. Even those who haven't read the book may be familiar with it through one or more of the films and plays it has inspired. Over 100 editions have been printed in many languages (Wright 1979, 32), and in the century and a quarter since it was originally published the book has won critical acclaim and become a children's classic. It remains available today in formats ranging from elaborately bound and illustrated editions to inexpensive paperbacks.

The Writing of *Hans Brinker*

In 1865 Dodge began to write a short children's serial for Tilton's *Independent*. She had already read Motley's *The Rise of the Dutch Republic*, a long, detailed historical work that had been recommended to readers of the *Working Farmer*. And she plunged so enthusiastically into more research on the subject that her short serial soon grew into quite a long book. Her New Jersey neighbors the Scharffs, who had lived in Holland, generously supplied her not only with information on the Dutch background but also with the story of Raff Brinker. Dodge took care to thank "these kind Holland friends" as she acknowledged in her preface other "obligations to many well known writers on Dutch history, literature, and art" (*HB*, preface).

Contemporary Reception of *Hans Brinker*

Since the *Independent* now found the story too long, Dodge submitted it to O'Kane, the publisher of her *Irvington Stories*, to whom she was committed for another book. O'Kane didn't want *Hans Brinker*, but Dodge, with sure judgment, pressed him to take it. The public was delighted with the book, and it became an immediate best-seller. In fact, in 1865 the only book with comparable sale figures was Charles Dickens's *Our Mutual Friend* (Wright 1979, 35), and in the years 1865–81 *Hans Brinker* received more reviews than any other children's book in the United States (Darling 1968, 229). Many of these reviews were the results of new editions of the novel; still, the number of those editions also attests to the book's reputation and genuine popularity.

In *Hans Brinker* Dodge created something new, a realistic story for children that broke with the heavy-handed didacticism of the earlier part of the nineteenth century. Its publishing history indicates that Dodge's story of young people caught in conflict between their duties to themselves and their familial and social responsibilities has a perennial appeal. A number of the early reviews praised the book for the naturalness of its characterization, an aspect that set it apart from other children's books of the time. Richard Darling has observed that "if Hans seems almost too good to be true to the modern reader," he must nevertheless have seemed real to a generation brought up on the Rollo books and he "paved the way for even more natural boys to come" (Darling 1968, 237).

Most early reviewers regarded the story's heavy cargo of information about Dutch history and customs as an attractive feature.

Indeed, one review, in the *Nation*, noted that the plot "is really incidental to most agreeable descriptions of Amsterdam, Haarlem, and Leyden, and the Hague; to scraps of Dutch history; to pictures of the general scenery, position, popular life, and manners of Holland; and to the instructive development of character in the hero and heroine." This reviewer thought the novel "good reading" and, commenting on Dodge's reputation for appealing to the real interests of young readers, asserted that she had produced "nothing better than this charming tale, alive with incident and action, adorned rather than freighted with useful facts, and moral without moralization."[2]

Critics commented on the wide audience for the book, the *Atlantic Monthly* claiming that while it was addressed to children, it might be read "with pleasure and profit by their elders."[3] One critic even expressed the opinion that should Dodge wish to write a "strictly legitimate novel" for adults, she would certainly be successful at it.[4]

The *Atlantic Monthly* praised Dodge's ability to convey "wholesome influences on the young heart and mind" without being overly preachy: "there is no formal moral, obtruding itself in set phrase. The lessons inculcated, elevated in tone, are in the action of the story and the feelings and aspirations of the actors."[5]

The considerable attention given to the book from the very first was especially impressive because it was originally published by a relatively obscure New York firm. But the book's popularity grew steadily, particularly after more attractive, illustrated editions were published by Scribner, Armstrong and by Charles Scribner's Sons. A reviewer for *Scribner's Monthly*, commenting on the 1873 edition with illustrations by Darley, Nast, and other well-known artists of the day, was highly complimentary and (not surprisingly, since *Scribner's Monthly* shared staff with *St. Nicholas Magazine*, then edited by Dodge) seemed to know a good deal about Dodge's philosophy of writing for children. This reviewer noted that "one of the charms of *Hans Brinker* is that it seems to be written by an author who has no ideal child in her mind; whom she seeks to interest and instruct; not even an ideal Real Child—that precious creature who is the bane of much of the finer sort of juvenile literature of our day."[6] The book was in fact praised for qualities close friends like Frank Stockton and Fayal Clarke frequently saw in Dodge herself: a natural, straightforward earnestness; unaffectedness; wit; vivacity; a genial warmth; and a fresh young spirit.

Recent Critical Perspectives

In 1979 Catharine Morris Wright saw the appeal of Dodge's novel this way: "Long, lively, informative, it was full of color and personalities and action. It was a catalogue of Dutch art and architecture, of daily habits, points of view, politics; it was guidebook, romance, tragedy. Above all, it was people—real, live, and close by—part of its readers' own world, an amazing mixture of intent and theme with hardly a facet left wanting" (Wright 1979, 32). Jerome Griswold in 1984 stressed the story's thematic concern with the danger of being carried away by turbulent emotion, especially anger. Unmistakable parallels exist between Dodge's own experience as the widow of a man presumed to have drowned himself in the stormy Atlantic and the plot of "a novel involving a mother that townspeople call 'Widow Brinker' and her two children who lost their father during an oceanic storm but later recovered him" (Griswold, 49). Griswold suggests that in *Hans Brinker* Dodge has written a story that invites a strong emotional response from its young readers and yet condemns giving way to such a response: "She provides abundant temptations to test her readers' resolve and seduces them to abandon it, thereby creating the juvenile version of the romance novel" (Griswold, 59).

Marilyn Kaye hailed *Hans Brinker* as a remarkable book for its time, citing Dodge's lack of dogmatism and her "open-minded, realistic approach to the human condition, and especially the state of childhood."[7] And Harriet Christy in 1988 agreed with Wright that though Dodge was much concerned with the Dutch background, on another level the story is "a straightforward, earnest, and simple account of ordinary people, without regard to nationality."[8]

Theme and Structure

"On a bright December morning long ago, two thinly clad children were kneeling upon the bank of a frozen canal in Holland" (*HB*, chap. 1). So begins *Hans Brinker; or, The Silver Skates*. Here in the opening pages of the novel, Hans and Gretel Brinker find they can't skate very far or very well on their crude, homemade wooden skates. Their ability to skate becomes a metaphor for their growing readiness to assume responsibility for their own lives. The novel, which begins with two half-frozen children adjusting skates that cannot take them far, is designed to show young readers how courage and endurance can win them the freedom of action they desire.

Dodge's lifelong concern with the shaping role of imagination and play in the moral and social development of children led her to create in her novels—as she did in *St. Nicholas Magazine*—what she called a "pleasure-ground" ("CM," 353), in which problems of growth and maturation could be explored in terms of quests to be undertaken, games to be played, races to be won, and puzzles and mysteries to be solved. Dodge used these ritual contests to symbolize the hazardous process of growing up—a process requiring that children disengage themselves from their parents, achieve a certain self-realization, establish new relationships with their peers, and integrate themselves within the larger society.

There comes a moment when children ready to assume the freedom that goes with adult responsibility must begin to see their parents' protective attitudes as constricting and oppressive. There is much that is painful for both children and parents in this situation, and it can be difficult to present to young readers whose experience of life is yet limited.

Dodge meets the needs of such readers in several imaginative and effective ways. The often sad and frightening story of the young Brinkers is contrasted with the experience of other children and their parents, whose stories are told in a more detached and stylized way. Dodge adopts a narrative style well calculated to appeal to her audience, and to the slow-moving, psychologically realistic story of Hans and Gretel Brinker she adds mythic, illustrative, and symbolic elements that clarify the meaning of their struggle toward autonomy. In particular, she makes interesting use of the history of Holland itself, the "land of pluck," whose people have traditionally embodied the kind of Spartan courage needed to bring her young protagonists safely through their period of trial and danger.

Parents and Children: The Three Plots

Hans Brinker presents three related stories, all of them involving families. The first tells of Dr. Boekman, the great Dutch surgeon whose unhappy son Laurens, acting reluctantly as his father's assistant, makes an error in compounding a drug for a patient. Ten years before the novel begins, Laurens flees the Netherlands, believing himself a murderer. He gives his silver watch and a farewell message for his father to the kind peasant who helps him on his way.

The second story is that of the family of Raff Brinker, the peasant who helps Laurens. Brinker suffers an accident while working on the dykes the night Laurens meets him. A severe head injury leaves him a helpless amnesiac, unable to communicate with his family and given to fits of violence. Dame Brinker cares for him tenderly, but without the family's savings—which Raff has hidden—she is forced to work very hard to make ends meet. For 10 years the Brinkers struggle along, hoping for some improvement in Raff's condition. Raff's daughter, Gretel, has to leave school and work tending geese, while his son, Hans, takes on a variety of odd jobs and tries his best to take his father's place. The family suffers not only from real poverty but from social rejection by many of their neighbors.

The part of the Brinker story that most grips young readers tells of the coming-of-age of the Brinker children, Gretel and Hans. When the novel begins, she is 12 and he is 15. It is time for them to begin to take an active role in determining the direction in which their lives will go. Hans decides, against his mother's advice, to seek further medical help for the father he has been told is a hopeless case. Gretel faces her very mixed feelings toward her father, the pain of being a social outcast, and her own deep desire to achieve, and she begins to dream of winning the skating race that has caught the imagination of all the young people in Broek. Hans's generosity and self-sacrifice impress Dr. Boekman, who is persuaded to treat Raff's head injury. Once cured, Raff remembers where he hid the family fortune and—conveniently— is able to deliver the message Laurens Boekman had left for his father 10 years before. Because Gretel has had the courage to reach out for what she wants, Dr. Boekman can be reunited with his son, whose address is inscribed on the case of the silver skates she wins.

Hans Brinker may be experienced by young readers as a relatively accessible and unthreatening text. But Dodge's interest in themes of doubleness and the divided self and her refusal to underrate the risks and real costs of interpersonal commitment lend the novel a subversive moral ambiguity. Dodge does not ignore the dark side of the psyche, but she handles potentially traumatic situations with sufficient detachment to make them bearable for young readers. Like many authors of the late nineteenth century, she uses literary doubles to explore the conflict-laden emotional situation of growing up.

If Hans Brinker is a somewhat idealized caregiver whose choices are unfailingly noble and selfless, Gretel is a repository of many of the inadmissible feelings young people may have as they struggle to free themelves from the domination of even the most loving parents. Gretel is allowed to feel weakness, resentment, fear, anger, hatred of a father she thinks she should love, anxiety that she won't be able to achieve what others achieve, and a great deal of guilt. In exploring the responses of both the disciplined Hans and the more volatile and sensitive Gretel as they struggle through their inevitable rites of passage, Dodge gives her young readers the comfort of catharsis together with the consolation of a happy ending.

Dodge's third story concerns a whole group of young people from the Brinkers' hometown of Broek who, like Hans and Gretel, face the challenges of adolescent life but whose experience—viewed in a more detached way—can more readily demonstrate the causal connection between right action and its consequences demanded by the moral economy of the novel. These young people are from more fortunate families than the Brinkers. They include the wealthy Peter van Holp and Hilda van Gleck (who intervene significantly in the Brinker story), as well as the prosperous peasant girl Annie Bauman, stout Jacob Poot, handsome Carl Schummel, and the English boy, Benjamin Dobbs.

Symbolic Action: Skating

The novel begins with the two Brinker children playing ice tag on squeaky wooden skates, "clumsy pieces of wood narrowed and smoothed at their lower edge, and pierced with holes, through which were threaded strings of rawhide" (*HB*, chap. 1). Those rawhide strings can hurt, and the children can't skate for very long before the damp wooden skates begin to trip them up. As Hans and Gretel begin to make significant choices for themselves—Hans deciding to ask Dr. Boekman's help and Gretel setting her heart on winning the race—they acquire better skates and move more effectively among the peers who have rejected them. Young readers may not appreciate exactly why Hans makes a series of difficult, selfless choices, culminating in his decision to become a surgeon. But the cost of a life of service to others will be brought home to them, vividly, when Hans sells his skates to buy medicine for his father or lends a skate strap to Peter at a crucial moment in the race. And they will appreciate why Peter, the winner, feeling that Hans has won a moral victory of sorts, attempts to give him the silver skates Peter himself has won—a gesture Hans, of course, refuses.

Though Gretel is the best skater among the young girls of Broek, she shivers in a thin jacket and stumbles on homemade skates. But Gretel is empowered by Hilda van Gleck, who generously gives her a warm jacket and good skates, and invites her to compete in the great race. The effect of Hilda on Gretel's life is pointed up in a significant incident. Closed out of the family discussions about the operation to be performed on her father, Gretel understands little of what is happening and looks on in terror as the doctor begins his work. She flees the cottage in tears, and when

Hilda finds Gretel asleep outside in the cold, she shakes her awake and, by forcing her to move, saves her from freezing to death. Later, encouraged by Hilda, Gretel wins the race and is crowned "Queen of the Skaters."

It is not surprising to find, by the conclusion of the novel, that Gretel has begun to model her own life on that of the girl who has befriended her, becoming not only "the finest singer, the loveliest woman in Amsterdam," "the dearest sister ever known," "the brightest, sweetest little wife in Holland" but also a woman whose kindness to the poor makes the air "fill with blessings" (*HB*, "Conclusion"). Lest the reader forget the depths of despair from which Gretel rose to attain this full self-realization, however, the very last image in the book is an evocation of "a tiny form trembling and sobbing on the mound before the Brinker cottage," "the darling little girl who won the silver skates" (*HB*, "Conclusion").

Symbolic Action: The Quest

Peter and Hans are of an age, and, like Gretel, Peter serves as a double for Hans. Both boys are intelligent, generous, and brave, but Peter is a free agent, unconstrained by poverty and misfortune. In the middle of the novel the narrative of the Brinkers' story breaks off—for 21 chapters—while the reader is told in great detail of the skating trip taken by Peter and his friends to The Hague. Dodge uses this trip to introduce many stories from Dutch history that serve as parables to teach the virtues needed to survive in a dangerous world. But the events of the skating trip are also a kind of miniature quest in which "Captain Peter" proves his leadership and his heroism. Significantly, when Peter loses the travel money entrusted to him, it is Hans Brinker, skating to Leyden to find Dr. Boekman, who returns it and makes it possible for the trip to be finished. In turn, it is Peter who volunteers to complete Hans's mission so that he can return to help his mother and sister with the now-seriously-ill Raff Brinker.

The skating trip has often been seen by critics as "disruptive" to the story and essentially nothing more than a "travelogue" in which "every sight becomes an excuse for conversations in which accounts of historical events, noted personages in Dutch history, and significant aspects of Dutch culture are discussed in great detail" (Kaye, 292; cf. Griswold, 47–48). Aside from its other rhetorical and dramatic functions, however, the skating trip offers an opportunity for the young boys (and especially Hans's alter ego, Peter) to play out the familiar fairy-tale drama in which the young separate from the family, go out into the world, face and overcome symbolic obstacles to their growth, and achieve the wisdom necessary to their final happiness.

Unlike the overbearing Dr. Boekman, who failed to respect his son's need to find his own way in life, or the violent and unreasoning Raff Brinker, whose brutal moods threaten to destroy his family, the parents of Peter and his friends are warm, supportive figures who have encouraged their sons to skate to Leyden and have paid their travel expenses. Peter and the boys easily meet the dangers and challenges of their symbolic journey to autonomy, for in the fairy-tale world of the skating trip their every effort is blessed with providential good fortune.

The incidents of the journey test Peter's prudence, generosity, and courage, as he must deal with a lost purse, the sickness of a friend, and a murderous thief (perhaps suggestive of the dark side of his own father) who threatens the boys as they sleep. Having met these challenges and having been instructed in the brave and responsible traditions of his people, Peter is rewarded by being able to stay for two days at The Hague in the home of his sister and her husband, Mevrouw and Mynheer van Gend. The van Gends' home is described as "a royal resting place," and as Peter approaches it he is like "a knight, an adventurer, travel-soiled and weary, a Hop-o'-my Thumb grown large, a Fortunatus approaching the enchanted castle" (*HB*, chap. 26). A spell of quiet hangs over the house; the servants are described as genies, Peter's sister as a sleeping beauty, and her conservatory as a "Garden of Delight" (*HB*, chap. 27). Each boy has his heart's desire and is provided with a private room, a space of his own. "Every boy his own chrysalis" is their motto, suggesting that this stay at the van Gends will be an occasion for growth and transformation, the boys' well-earned rest a participation in the restorative magic of the place (*HB*, chap. 27).

The young couple are idealized quasi-parental figures who can support, amuse, and entertain the boys without pressure or coercion. After a stay in their home, the boys are refreshed and ready to return to Broek. It is perhaps significant that their journey home is without untoward incident. They skate like champions and return in triumph. Far from being a distracting digression, the journey to The Hague is an effective device to bring home to the younger reader the essential message of *Hans Brinker*: that the adolescent crisis of separation from the family can, when negotiated successfully, lead to a reconciliation with the family that renders both parents and children capable of living a fuller life.

Symbolic Action: Carnival

Dodge used parties and festive occasions to symbolize the happy possibilities that flow from allowing the joyous spirit of carnival to transform a life that may have hardened into a constricting routine. In story after story of hers, characters are drawn together in a spirit of "joyful relativity"[9] in which rigid and negative attitudes can be thrown off, hierarchical barriers set aside. And in Dodge's fiction characters who enter even briefly into this "life lived inside out" (Bakhtin, 8:122) are empowered to make permanent, life-enhancing changes in terms of their everyday circumstances. Dodge's favorite image of the good life is, of course, the holiday she loved best, Christmas. And references to Christmas and to St. Nicholas pervade her work.

In *Hans Brinker* the frozen canals of Broek teem with skaters, young and old, rich and poor, drawn together in the spirit of carnival presided over by the good St. Nicholas, the children's saint. It is midwinter, not only Christmastide but also the winter solstice, a period of traditional saturnalian festivity. It is a time of magic reversals of ordinary circumstance, a time when long-hidden secrets can be revealed, puzzles can be solved, the "dead" like Raff Brinker can be brought back to life, and a goosegirl can be crowned "Queen of the Skaters."

When the narrative pauses over a typical Dutch St. Nicholas Eve celebration in the van Gleck home (*HB*, chap. 9), readers are invited to enter a magical moment out of time in which such thematic concerns as the relationship of children to their parents can be dealt with in a symbolic way. The celebration is a warm family affair notwithstanding the tensions between parents as lawgivers, judges, and teachers and the children who are their dependents, novices at the game of life who need instruction, who almost always fall short of perfection, and who are liable to punishment and criticism. It is holiday time, however, a time when judgment can be tempered with mercy and when young and old can come together in a brief utopian truce.

Though Dodge is often classified as a literary realist, there is a strong streak of fantasy in the novel, as there tends to be whenever fiction treats of carnival themes. When Peter and his friends set out on their skating holiday, they encounter a woman who looks "like a scare-thaw invented by old father Winter for the protection of his skating grounds" (*HB*, chap. 19). They are entranced by iceboats that float by like great swans. It is the master of one of these boats, puffing like a genie on his pipe, who claims he goes where the wind blows him and offers the boys a lift. Their ride is an enchanted flight into a fairy-tale world where they can become storybook heroes: "The boys felt very much as Sinbad had when tied to the Roc's leg, he darted through the clouds; or as Bellerophon felt when he shot through the air on the back of his winged horse Pegasus" (*HB*, chap. 19). Even within the relatively realistic Brinker plot there is a strong fantasy component. The finding of the treasure that Raff Brinker had buried for safekeeping before he was injured, for example, is told as a kind of parodic fairy tale, with magic incantations and gestures, and a presiding "good fairy" in the person of Annie Baumann, who taps the ground and tells Hans where to dig.

At the heart of the carnival experience, of course, is a unifying ritual performance into which everyone can be drawn. Throughout the novel, everyone in Broek looks forward to the great race. When it has been played out, all the skaters form into a great procession that snakes, like a living creature, in and out of the "gaily twined" arches that have been erected on the ice (*HB*, chap. 44). For a moment all are united. The buoyant spirit of holiday

time made so vivid here gives *Hans Brinker* much of the charm
and vitality that have made it so popular, but the concept of
carnival also includes an awareness that the unity of the holiday
time is brief. The procession breaks up, and the skaters scatter
across the ice. At the end of the novel, when the later lives of the
various boys and girls of Broek who have skated in that race are
detailed, there is—as always in carnivalistic fiction—a touch of
pathos, a recognition that time brings change and losses—for
some early; for everyone, sooner or later.

Narrative Technique

For the 1873 edition of the book Dodge supplied "A Letter from
Holland" to introduce the story to the "Dear Boys and Girls at
Home." The letter serves to highlight Dodge's treatment of a country "full of oddity, courage, and industry—the pluckiest little
country on earth," but an even more important function of it is to
introduce the "auntly voice" of the storyteller,[10] a voice Dodge
deliberately intended to make "familiar and chatty," even at the
risk of seeming a bit long-winded.[11]

The narrative simulates an oral presentation of the story to a
group of children ranging in age from 8 to 15. Many of the distinctive features of Dodge's style are dictated by this manner of telling
the story. Its massive amplification of detail is designed not only
to "bind" a good deal of "lore"[12] but to illustrate central themes,
like the need for courage and endurance. Its "empathetic and
participatory" manner stimulates reader identification with the
characters' experience and heightens the pathos of a scene like
Gretel's flight from the cottage or the excitement of one like the
great race (Ong, 45). Flat, stylized characters—the anxious
mother, the sensitive daughter, the stalwart son, the gruff but
kind physician—are described in repeated phrases that acquire
a formulaic force. We hear much of "Captain Peter," "Good Saint
Nicholas," "little Voostenwalbert." And a number of characters
with whom the reader is invited to sympathize are termed
"poor"—"poor little Gretel," "poor Jacob," "poor Laurens."

The vignettes from Dutch history recounted during the story are sometimes brutal. But the oral tradition often presents physical conflict and includes extensive description of violent behavior (Ong, 44). Such passages certainly seize the attention and fix lessons in the memory of even unskilled readers or listeners. The constant praise of Dutch endurance in the face of invasion, hardship, and natural disaster might seem overdone to sophisticated tastes, but fulsome praise is part of the oral tradition, too, and "goes with the highly polarized, agonistic, oral world of good and evil, virtue and vice, villains and heroes" (Ong, 45). As in the oral tradition, the moral lessons to be drawn from incidents in the narrative are often presented in the pithy, easy-to-remember form of proverbs, such as those attributed to Jacob Cats.

Many modern writers of realistic fiction for children work in terms of "exact correspondence between the linear order of elements in discourse and the referential order, the chronological order in the world to which the discourse refers" (Ong, 147). But Dodge's storyteller ranges freely over the "facts" and relates the tale topically, rather than chronologically. For example, in chapter 4, just after Peter van Holp has ordered a wooden necklace for his sister from Hans, readers are told, "Two days afterward, on Saint Nicholas Eve, Hans, having burned three candle, ends, and cut his thumb into the bargain, stood in the market place at Amsterdam, buying another pair of skates" (*HB*, chap. 4). Ordinarily, one might expect that when the narrative pickes up again, it would be after the skates had been bought, but the description of Hans buying the skates turns out to be a quick flash-forward. A great deal of important action must take place between the time Hans gets the order for the necklace and the time he buys the skates at the end of chapter 7. Similarly, chapter 41 tells how Hans finds the family treasure one night; only in the next chapter do we discover that something equally interesting has happened earlier that day: Raff has begun to remember how Laurens entrusted him with the silver watch that has been a mystery throughout the story. Because of the strong topical continuity the narrative maintains at each of the time shifts involved, the effect is not jarring and seems quite natural.

The lengthy digression concerning the skating expedition to The Hague has often been singled out as a weakness by critics. But even apart from its important thematic and psychological functions in the story, this digression may work better for readers less oriented than most adults are toward the ultimate satisfactions of the linear plot. The skating-trip interlude is also well designed to present information efficiently to the reader, treating historical material in short units that reiterate the same thematic message. The visits to museums and art galleries reprise the historical anecdotes and help to fix them in memory through "object lessons." Though modern readers may find the mass of information conveyed here wearisome, Dodge was working within an established genre—the educational travel story—for which contemporary readers were prepared, and all the background information is conceptualized and verbalized "with more or less close reference to the human lifeworld, assimilating the alien, objective world to the more immediate familiar interaction of human beings" (Ong, 42).

Some of the tricks Dodge plays with narrative sequence are not quite so successfully managed. Chapter 8, for example, ends with Hans hearing his mother scream. The reader already knows she is probably in grave danger, but chapter 9 doesn't continue with the Brinkers' story; instead, the anxious reader is offered a chapter-long digression on a St. Nicholas Eve celebration. As Jerome Griswold has pointed out, throughout the novel Dodge "creates emotional situations and then urges control" (Griswold, 59). This offering of a sudden diversion in chapter 9 is a familiar—though here not very satisfactory—Dodge device to provide emotional relief from a tense situation. For many modern readers (Kaye, for example), such digressions are "incongruous" (Kaye, 292) and break the story's narrative momentum. Perhaps the only merit in the sudden shift of scene is the reminder offered by chapter 9 that a world where bounty makes life sweet exists side by side with the dark little cottage where St. Nicholas does not come.

The "auntly" narrator's perspective on the action shifts from moment to moment for rhetorical advantage. The storyteller sometimes seems to know the future but at other times is merely a witness, looking on at a scene with the reader and wondering what will happen next, or where the skaters will go when they skate out of view. Now and then the storyteller will even express surprise at some event, or satisfaction at not having hazarded a guess about an unexpected turn of plot. This "auntly voice," with its disarmingly frank admission that it doesn't know everything, is a rhetorically persuasive device designed to win ready acceptance for the judgments it *does* make.

Hans Brinker is in a sense a travel book, but it is also a piece of speculative fiction in which Holland offers an alternative moral landscape designed to make readers think critically about their own ethical world. The Dutch national character is presented as an ideal to which Americans might aspire. These passive-looking folk are described as braver than anyone else in their ability to achieve ultimate victory—not by being aggressive and warlike but through their patient, principled resistance to the oppressor and their unrelenting struggle against the angry waters of the sea. They are praised for their art, music, and literature; their intellectual and technical achievements; and their "important discoveries and inventions," "learning" and "science" (*HB*, chap. 2). But they are also notable for the industry and flair for business that has made them excel at commerce and for the curiosity and sense of adventure that have made them famous navigators. Their "promotion of education and public charities" and "the money and labor" they expend on public works are described as noble examples to the rest of the world (*HB*, chap. 2).

Throughout the novel, the narrative voice first presents characters in action and then provides privileged knowledge of their interior dispositions so that an inexperienced reader can know how to take what they say. An admirable character like Peter can then be used to teach young readers how to interpret a situation or understand someone's behavior. For example, Peter makes clear his belief that how one is brought up can determine one's character, saying to his friends of the thief he has caught, "He is my brother, and yours too. . . . We cannot say what we might have become under other circumstances. . . . A happy home and good parents might have made that man a fine fellow instead of what he is" (*HB*, chap. 23). And Peter's brother-in-law, a man of wisdom and authority, is used to make the point that "all the world over women have never been found wanting in their country's hour of trial, . . . though . . . [our] own countrywomen stand foremost in the records of female patriotism and devotion" (*HB*, chap. 27). On the other hand, young Rychie Korbes, who is shown to be selfish and thoughtless, is taken to task for feeling that the "poor could toil and labor at a respectable distance" from people of her class but should aspire to nothing higher, and her personal motto— "[I]f they rebel, put them down; if they suffer, don't trouble me about it" (*HB*, chap. 15)—clearly epitomizes an attitude readers are invited to reject.

The "auntly voice" directly commends the Dutch for their commitment to religious freedom and calls the country "the asylum of the world," "for the oppressed of every nation have there found shelter and encouragement" (*HB*, chap. 2). And when young Ben Dobbs finds the worshipers in a Dutch church "outrageous" and "sinful" because they don't take their hats off, the narrator comments, "There is an angel called Charity who often would save our hearts a great deal of trouble if we but let her in." The Christian world is said to be "one, after all, however divided by sects and differences it may be" (*HB*, chap. 29), but there are limits to this tolerant attitude: some comments on the Inquisition drew a protest from the *Catholic World* when the book first appeared (Darling 1968, 230), and the regrettable observation that Ben Dobbs "*wisely* resolved to keep away from "the Jewish Quarter of Amsterdam [our italics]" reflects the anti-Semitic bias of the time (*HB*, chap. 10).

The narrative voice of *Hans Brinker* draws conclusions, raises questions, and provides significant support to inexperienced readers. As in the oral tradition, it can carry readers into digressive interludes without losing their attention or frustrating them, especially when the particular unit of narrative is structured around a game, contest, journey, or ritual with its own intrinsic satisfactions. Dodge's frequent digressions into history and travelogue— often seen as narrative flaws in the novel—structure the child's reading of the story, providing relief from scenes of emotional intensity and offering important clues to the meaning of situations and relationships that may be outside the young reader's experience. Thus, the numerous stories of brave citizens under siege suggest the desperate situation of the Brinkers and the qualities they need to endure and survive, and the stories of the Hero of Haarlem, the long skating trip to Amsterdam, and the race for the silver skates are all informed by the same themes of threat and endurance, self-sacrifice and triumph that resound throughout the novel as a whole.

The Hero of Haarlem

One of the best-loved set pieces in *Hans Brinker* is the fable about the little boy who saved Holland from a flood. The story is a simple but affecting one. A gentle, sunny-haired boy, son of a dykeman, comes home late and notices a leak in the dyke. The boy understands the danger at once and thrusts his finger in the hole. His first reaction is delight that he has stopped the "angry waters." But soon other feelings come: cold, dread, fear, numbness, pain. The boy prays for help and resolves—despite his terror and his feeling that he might not survive the night—to stay at his post until morning, when indeed help does come (*HB*, chap. 18).

The story is imbedded in a chapter of the novel that raises the questions, Are people really brave and noble? and What is an appropriate response to semilegendary stories of selfless heroism? The members of Peter's skating party discuss and debate these issues while they are skating "beside the Holland dyke" at Haarlem (*HB*, chap. 18). The group includes an English boy, Benjamin Dobbs, to whom Dutch history, language, and culture are new and strange. Ben's little brother and sister, Robby and Jenny, have not visited Holland, but by a feat of authorial sleight of hand, Dodge arranges matters so that at the very moment Ben is skating through Haarlem, Robby and Jenny, back in England, stand "ready to join in the duties of their reading class," which is about to read the story of the little Dutch hero. The children in the English schoolroom are required to roar out "at schoolroom pitch"

"Lesson 62. THE HERO OF HAARLEM." Jenny Dobbs takes her turn in reading the story aloud, and as the hero's situation becomes more painful and dangerous, her voice begins to falter with emotion. She is told by a stern and unsympathetic schoolmaster, "[I]f you cannot control your feelings so as to read distinctly, we will wait until you recover yourself" (*HB*, 18).

Jenny's unquestioning belief in the possibility of human nobility and her emotional response to the story of the little hero of Haarlem are confirmed as appropriate in a conversation the skaters have (coincidentally, at the same moment the children in England are reading the tale). Ben says he has heard the story before but only now realizes it is true. Lambert insists it is known to be true all over Holland, and reaffirms the lesson of the piece by adding, "[T]hat little boy represents the spirit of the whole country. Not a leak can show itself anywhere either in its politics, honor, or public safety, that a million fingers are not ready to stop it at any cost" (*HB*, chap. 18).

The little hero of Haarlem is in essence very like Hans and Peter, and his story is so perfectly adapted to Dodge's purpose that it might easily be supposed she created it herself. But though the story has been attributed to Dodge by scholars (Wright 1979, 89; Griswold, 59; Kaye, 293), it is not original. In 1855 Beeton's *Boy's Own Magazine* presented a story called "The Little Dutch Hero" that, paragraph for paragraph and sometimes phrase for phrase, tells the same story. ("Dutch Hero," 293–94). No author is listed for this version, which predates Dodge's by 10 years. But in 1871 there appeared in *Old Merry's Annual* a similar piece, called "The Little Dykeman," said to be translated from the French of Madame Eugénie Foa ("Dykeman," 638–40). It would seem likely, from a comparative reading, that the *Boy's Own Magazine* version and the Dodge version stem from the same original source as "The Little Dykeman."

Dodge never discussed the provenance of this little story, perhaps because she believed it to be in the public domain, as were the historical anecdotes she retold. Its appearance in a school reader within the text and the insistence on its historicity by the Dutch characters in the story suggest Dodge was not trying to claim any special originality for it. What is original, however, is the way she uses it. Within the novel many exemplary stories are presented to model audiences of varied ages, backgrounds, and experiences. The privileged older boys of the skating party hear (and debate) stories from Motley that teach them what they need to know: what it means to be good, brave, and dutiful. Hans and Gretel, who already possess these virtues and who need hope, hear instead the legend of St. Nicholas, giver of second chances at life, of largesse and of happy endings. Ben's little brother and sister read a story that reduces the heroic tales from Motley to childsize, for they—and the youngest readers of Dodge's novel, who will identify with them—need to know that they, too, can in their everyday life be brave—like its nameless young hero.

The courage needed by ordinary children to meet the challenges of ordinary life is a recurrent theme in Dodge's work. Dodge felt that children's fiction should cultivate the child's imagination, should give pleasure, and should stimulate ambition, but she also believed that it should prepare children for life as it is. And life, as Dodge had come to know through tragic personal experience, is not always easy. The happy ending of *Hans Brinker* is bitterly hard won, and many of her characters sustain real—and irrevocable—losses.

The full title of Dodge's novel, *Hans Brinker; or, The Silver Skates*, epitomizes the ambiguity of the experience Dodge explores in it. The adolescent quest for independence and self-realization can be painful. Hans does not win the silver skates but sacrifices his chance in much the same way he has sacrificed many opportunities to practice for the race. And Gretel's victory is hard won, the symbolic reward of a difficult inner journey toward maturity and reconciliation with her father. Yet, without denying the reality of pain and loss in the lives of her protagonists, Dodge suggests that the adolescent struggle for autonomy can be successfully achieved and can bring precious rewards. She supplements the Brinker's story with illustrative and symbolic elements that clarify the meaning of their struggle and bring home effectively to the younger reader that personal myth of endurance rewarded by victory which is her essential message.

5

Play, Games, and Poetry

In anyone's "intellectual life there are only a few topics, only a limited set of persistent queries and themes" that in retrospect give continuity to the whole.[1] Widowed under tragic and disturbing circumstances, Dodge was preoccupied by the problem of how best to deal with loss and disappointment. A lover of children, she spent much time and energy writing for them and trying to find literature and art that might teach, amuse, and inspire them. A devoted mother, she sought to share with other parents the methods she had used to make her own sons self-directed and eager learners. An essentially social person, she loved games and play, taking much delight in bringing people together to share their talents and enjoy themselves, whether at one of her evenings at home or through the pages of her periodicals.

In the pursuit of these interests, Dodge adopted a variety of roles that combined, in a curious way, a childlike innocence, spontaneity, and playfulness with "the cultivation of competence almost to the point of guile" (Bruner, 37). And gradually she developed around each of these roles a personal mythology. Dodge chose to see herself as the plucky descendant of Dutch forbears whose cheerful optimism, simple religious faith, intelligence, and devotion to duty would carry her through the darkest hours. Her fiction often focused on the virtues symbolized for her in the brave people of Holland and made memorable by her own pictures of

Hans Brinker and the little hero of Haarlem. Moreover, she focused some of her more popular poetry for adults specifically on the problem of making the best of difficult situations.

Not surprisingly for the daughter of an agricultural reformer, Dodge came to see herself as a kind of utopian landscape architect. Her favorite metaphor for the ideal children's magazine was the "pleasure ground." She saw the garden she would build for children as a place of their own, where they could have things their own way and learn through free and delighted play. And her poems for both children and adults speak often of what she called in one poem "The Grass World" (*AW*, 75) of an agreeably humanized natural space.

Dodge also played the part of the perfect mother—nurturing and tender, but also an ideal playfellow to her children, a comrade who could enter into their games and studies with zest. Some of the occasional poems she wrote for family birthday celebrations express with more feeling than art the intense, almost-overwhelming affection she felt for her own sons. But her unusual ability to emphasize with children more often helped her to avoid such sentimentality. Her "Jack-in-the Pulpit" persona, which gave a human touch to the editorial pieces in *St. Nicholas,* owes much to her image of herself as an idealized parent-teacher-friend.

As the presiding genius of a magazine named for the patron saint of children and embodying the festive spirit, generous sociality, and bounty associated with her favorite holiday, Dodge became a kind of cultural icon: "Mrs. Dodge," the "Conductor" of *St. Nicholas*. In this very public role she was the expert editor, friend of the famous, bringer of good things, mistress of the revels. From the very beginning of her writing career, Christmas was prominent as a theme of stories, articles, and verses; indeed, it became a sort of personal signature theme for Dodge.

Play

In fact, festive occasions of all kinds abound in Dodge's fiction: birthday parties, club meetings, masquerades, holiday celebra-

tions, a house picnic, dolls' tea parties, parlor theatricals. Over
and over again, she describes moments when people come together
to enjoy themselves, social situations where there are no specta-
tors: all are participants in the happy activity of the occasion,
freed from everyday rules and strictures, including etiquette. In-
dividuals are drawn into familiar contact and allowed to express
their hidden feelings and ideas, to cross social barriers and forge
new relationships. On such occasions there is a delight in absur-
dity, nonsense, a humorous upside-down perspective on things.
Above all, there is a willingness to look at the world playfully,
"as one great communal performance" (Bakhtin, 8:160). Dodge's
many pieces about parties and games celebrate the value of such
experiences. And this openness and sociality are also characteristic of the magazine she created. Though *St. Nicholas* certainly
had a didactic agenda, young readers did not find the magazine
oppressive, perhaps because at its heart it offered a subversive,
imaginative vision of a world open to change. As Bakhtin says of
the carnival spirit in literature, "This sense of the world, liberat-
ing one from fear, bringing the world maximally close to a person
and bringing one person maximally close to another (everything
is drawn into the zone of free familiar contact), with its joy at
change and its joyful relativity, is opposed to that one-sided and
gloomy official seriousness which is dogmatic and hostile to evolu-
tion and change, which seeks to absolutize a given condition of
existence or a given social order" (Bakhtin, 8:160). Dodge believed
with Froebel that "the organization of childish play should be
the first culture of the mind ("Kindergarten," 258). Growth and
learning should slip in among the pleasures the child naturally
seeks, and schooling should be an opportunity to extend a process
of discovery begun freely through play. Like her friends Louisa
May Alcott, Mark Twain, and Robert Louis Stevenson, Dodge
often chose to describe children's play in her fiction. Her treatment
of imaginative play suggests she saw it as sometimes opening up
novel and risky—but ultimately rewarding—lines of action. "The
Hermit of the Hills," for example, begins by describing the transgressions committed by a group of playful children on a reclusive
old man's privacy. The children are afraid of yet fascinated by

him, and their ever-bolder invasion of his space, imaged as a
military operation, initiates the story's action. In "Po-no-kah," too,
it is an initial period of play in the forest that tempts the Hedden
children to explore even more dangerous territory. The central
issue in "Capt. George, the Drummer-Boy" turns on the difference
between pretending to be a soldier and really being one; the story
begins with imitative soldier play that projects the young hero
into a situation in which he is asked to enlist in an actual war.

Like Twain, Dodge could describe very convincingly the way children interact in play groups. In "A Garret Adventure" she has great
fun with the story of a mischievous and bored group of children
confined to an attic on a snowy day. Their fooling around is realistically described, and the mischief culminates in their decision to
build a skating pond there, with predictably comic results as water
drips through the ceilings below. Sometimes Dodge seems to suggest
that the way a child plays says something about his or her moral
nature. In "The Golden Gate" the play styles of two little girls define
their moral characters. And in "Cushamee" it is a refusal of doll play
with his sister that brings Tom Laffer a demonic dream-visitation
from a doll bent on exacting retribution for his unkindness.

Games

In her novels Dodge sometimes used games metaphorically.
Skating in *Hans Brinker* symbolizes the way one lives one's life.
In *Donald and Dorothy* the games played at a house party say
something about each player's approach to life. Sometimes game-
playing represents an individual's attempt to master adverse circumstances: motherless Dorothy Reed in *Donald and Dorothy*
dresses up in the old clothes of a beloved aunt and cradles the
aunt's doll. Sometimes play is used to find a solution to a vexing
problem: Fandy Danby in the same book wants very much to
control his friends and his siblings, and so he challenges them to
play aggressive games he thinks he can win, and preaches to them
make-believe sermons on their misdeeds. Sometimes play tests
strength, or prepares a young person for the future: Donald Reed

practices his marksmanship until he is expert enough to win a
shooting match; the real prize, though, is not the trinket he wins
but the skill with which he is able to defend his sister and his
friends against a mad dog.

Dodge enjoyed parlor games and copyrighted two successful
commercial games herself. *The Stratford Game* was based on quotations from Shakespeare, but Dodge credited her 10-year-old son
Harry with the idea for it. *The Protean Cards* was an attractively
packaged set of cards that could be used in ingenious ways. One
of Dodge's first assignments for Horace Scudder's *Riverside Magazine for Young People* called on her special interest in children's
amusements. "Holiday Whispers concerning Games and Toys,"
dealing with what was available in New York's toy stores, appeared just before Christmas in the issue for January 1867. In
this piece Dodge urged parents to purchase for their children toys
that would engage them in active play. "The aesthetic needs of
childhood should by no means be ignored; but beware," she said,
"how you trifle with the divine instinct that prefers a hammer to
a flower" ("Holiday Whispers," 41). She suggested such toys as
microscopes, printing presses, dolls that had to be dressed, puzzles, magic lanterns and optical devices called Zoetropes. And she
pointed out that opticians or scientific supply stores could provide
other items that would arouse the child's curiosity and interest:
magnets, burning glasses, pocket compasses, telescopes, simple
electric motors, and gyroscopes. Although Dodge felt shy about
singling out her own game for special praise, her business sense
prevailed and she compromised with her conscience by quoting a
friend's praise for *The Protean Cards*.

In Scudder's *Riverside* the "game" article was a familiar genre,
and Dodge soon developed a specialty: the amusing, smoothly
written account of an entertaining set of party games or holiday
festivities designed to serve readers as inspiration and resource
for their own home entertainment. "Kaleidoscopes and Burglars"
and "Bessie's Birthday Party" provided a light fictive setting for
the detailed description of games and entertainments suitable for
a children's party. Some of the shadow plays and dramatic charades Dodge described were quite elaborate. Though home theat-

ricals had been disapproved of earlier in the century, by the 1850s many articles offering advice about staging and scripting such events had begun to appear. Dodge's own family had enjoyed such home performances when she was growing up,[2] and she was able to supply precise and lively scripts to follow in her *Riverside* pieces.

Capitalizing on her knowledge of games, Dodge in 1869 produced an odd and original little book called *A Few Friends and How they Amused Themselves: A Tale in Nine Chapters Containing Descriptions of Twenty Pastimes and Games and a Fancy Dress Party*. At Robert Owen's suggestion, she submitted the manuscript to J. B. Lippincott and Company in Philadelphia, which wanted it for holiday issue (Wright 1979, 49). In this work Dodge advocated games to arouse pleasurable excitement and develop cohesiveness in small social groups. Her purpose, acknowledged in the preface, was to "present, in narrative form, a number of pastimes and intellectual games which persons of culture may enjoy, and which may also serve to bring young folk and their seniors together in a common pursuit of pleasure and profit" (*FF*, 1). Although "society in its crude, dressy state is indeed apt to disdain all pastimes of fancy and wit" (*FF*, 7), Dodge asserted that the one human distinguishing trait is the ability to play games (*FF*, 6). Adopting the persona of a hostess eager to prevent ennui from ruining her social evening, she offered a wry description of guests "enlivened, or rather deadened, by a fell purpose not to enjoy themselves" (*FF*, 11).

In *A Few Friends* all of the wrong people have gathered in little groups "like so many icy stalagmites" (*FF*, 12), and not until the hostess's friend Henry Stykes exerts considerable charm, humor, and ingenuity to organize games does the party succeed. Three guessing games are described in detail, and illustrated through a narrative of the guests at play. The characters of the players are revealed in the ways in which they compete, and the excitement generated saves both the evening and the hostess's sanity.

Delighted with the results of this kind of entertainment, the guests determine to meet every fortnight for the rest of the season to pursue their game plan. Dubbing themselves the Child-again

Society, they meet in one another's homes, from mansion to rented room, and engage in varied entertainments: 14 guessing games in the style of Twenty Questions, 5 activities requiring elaborate props and settings (including a fancy dress party), and 5 writing games.

Some of these games involve simple devices, such as attempting to make participants laugh, guessing voices, and using absurd hand gestures; others call on a knowledge of history, art, or literature. "Who Was He?" poses questions about the lives and works of historical figures, such as Michelangelo, Tasso, the Roman matron Arria, John Wilkes, and Mirabeau. "Quotations and Authors" draws on sources ranging from Shakespeare down through many lesser lights, chiefly British, of the nineteenth century. "Charades" necessitates the development of an elaborate dramatic script several pages long, reproduced in toto, the acting of which is described with considerable verve.

The formal code of social behavior sanctioned by the genteel tradition enforced distinctions of class, gender, and age, limiting social interaction at parties; however the right sorts of games and play could free guests from the rigidities of convention. The games Dodge suggests allow participants to escape from prescribed behaviors and to act out in aggressive and competitive ways. They offer challenges to skill and intelligence, a chance to demonstrate physical or intellectual competence, and the satisfaction of winning. Dodge creates a host of characters who reveal hitherto-hidden aspects of their personalities as they enter into the games. For example, Mr. Simmons, a henpecked nouveau riche whose life has been given over to money-making, gets to comment on his wife's garrulity as she mimics a portrait and attempts to refrain from moving or laughing in the face of ingeniously contrived provocation from the other players. The suave Harry Stykes, who appoints himself master of ceremonies and cajoles compliance with the game rules, is driven to uncertainty and anxiety as he falls in love with Mary Glidden and pursues a decorous courtship throughout the biweekly meetings of the Child-again Society.

When the rules of the games have been spelled out, Dodge dramatizes the game-playing with its "lively spirit of good hu-

mored rivalry" (*FF*, 100). She stresses the intergenerational suitability of the entertainment by pointing out the ways games can
be adapted to children's level, "serving as an incentive to them as
well as a delightful vehicle of instruction, and . . . a capital school
of discipline for all" (*FF*, 80). She is also concerned that subject
matter for the games be not "inappropriately chosen" lest it cause
"pain and embarrassment." The entertainment and instructional
values of these pastimes must be wedded also to a moral rectitude
characterized as both innocent and kind (*FF*, 82). Competition
that permits a spirited one-upmanship is acceptable only when
limited by the demands of good taste and the gracious acceptance
of both success and defeat.

The game Dodge describes as "Lightning Poetry" may contain
a clue to her own attitudes toward versifying. The process involves
all participants writing subjects for poems on slips of paper. These
are collected, one is drawn from the pile, and 15 minutes are
allocated for each member of the group to compose an entry. They
protest the impossibility of the task, but Harry Stykes announces
that the secret is one of attitude: "Every man and woman here
can do it creditably when once a psychological circle is established
. . . [by] all concentrating ourselves on the same subject at the
same time" (*FF*, 144–45). This success, Dodge is careful to point
out, is judged, of course, by "the Lightning Poetry standard" (*FF*
151). The enthusiasm is such that the group members "began to
consider the highest and best condition of a mortal attained when,
with a pencil and paper at command, the most startling material,
never mind how refractory, was being subjugated into verse in
the shortest possible time" (*FF*, 159). When one member of the
group questions how they are able to complete the compositions
just in the allotted time, Harry answeres, "That's only a part of
the philosophy of the thing" (*FF*, 151).

In another version of the game, called "Lexidesma," each person
writes a "queer" word on one slip of paper and a question on
another. Then one of each is drawn from the pile, and the poets
are required to answer the question in verse, using the queer
word, in 10 minutes. Some of the resulting " 'poems' were as
dainty and pretty as they were ingenious; some were capable

specimens of the mock-heroic style, and some were good because they were so atrociously bad" (*FF*, 158). The volumes of verse that Dodge herself produced, some of which are quoted as achievements of the Child-again Society, indicate that she may have written under just such pressures and with such results as she filled out the issues of *Hearth and Home* or *St. Nicholas*.

Poetry

Dodge wrote verse all her life, with evident ease and delight. Popular in its day, her poetry remains interesting for what it suggests about her own ideas, attitudes, and values and for the way it places her in relation to certain other writers of the time—women poets, poets of the genteel tradition, and writers of verse for children. Many of Dodge's friends and colleagues commented on her ability to write verse on demand, with amazing speed. The knack stood her in good stead when a piece of "filler" was needed and the presses were waiting. But she made distinctions among the rhymes and jingles she turned out for the enjoyment of the child readers of *Hearth and Home* or *St. Nicholas*, the amusing light verse she wrote for adults, and the relatively fewer serious poems she was able to regard with any special satisfaction.

Dodge received much praise for her poetry from critics like E. C. Stedman, her work was published in prestigious magazines like the *Century*, and one or two of her poems—notably "The Two Mysteries" and "The Minuet"—became widely popular. But Dodge's head was not easily turned by flattery, and she clearly doubted the real worth of her serious poems. Dodge believed that true poets were rare and that their gift was mysterious and exalted. Her attitude toward poets she truly admired—such as Tennyson, Arnold, Emerson, Longfellow, and Whittier—was one of respect mixed with a sort of religious awe.

When her poem "The Two Mysteries" was published, Dodge received a flood of letters about it. "The Two Mysteries" is presented in the context of an epigraph describing an incident in the life of Walt Whitman. When his young nephew died, Whitman consoled a little girl who didn't seem to understand what had happened, saying "You don't know what it is, do you my dear?" and adding, "We don't either." In the poem Dodge picks up Whitman's remark and extends it by describing what death looks like and what "this desolate heart-pain," "the dread to take our daily way, and walk in it again" can feel like to the bereaved. She raises some of the questions that arise at such times: Where has the loved one gone? Why are we left behind? Why do we not understand? But the poet takes comfort in reflecting that we can't define life any more than we can define death, and that if one trusts in God it is possible to believe that "as life is to the living, so death is to the dead" (*AW*, 15–17).

Dodge was pleased at the response of the reading public to her poem but was also somewhat taken aback. She wrote to Longfellow in confidence explaining that she had heard praise of the poem from a number of literary people and—what interested her more—from "persons who had suffered bereavement." She seems to have suspected that these readers were reacting not so much to the poem but to "this treatment of the subject," for she asked him to read the verses and tell her "if they are good or not," adding, "I often write verses, but sometimes I wonder whether it is *right* for me to do so."[3] Dodge's qualms about "The Two Mysteries" may be explained by a bit of advice she gave in *St. Nicholas* to a child who had sent in some poetry: "Your verses are quite good considering your age. Beware of being too sentimental. God gives us some thoughts to hold and to live with, not to spin out in labored rhymes. That these thoughts will sometimes flash out, of themselves, in a true poet's verse, makes them all the more sacred. Never start out to write about them."[4]

Dodge clearly did not think that "The Two Mysteries" was a great poem, and she was troubled by the response suggesting that it was. Her self-doubts are a reminder that for many lovers of poetry in the nineteenth century, poems came in two kinds. Dodge's old friend the poet William Cullen Bryant distinguished between poems "acknowledged by the intelligent to be great," "and those which, 'though less perfect than others in form, have, by some power of touching the heart, gained and maintained a sure place in the popular esteem." For Bryant, the poetry of "common apprehension" written for "mankind at large . . . , near to the common track of the human intelligence" deserved the name of art as well as the more exalted work of "acknowledged masters."[5]

Though Dodge may have had few illusions about her poetry's merits, she was willing to allow it to be reprinted widely, and she responded graciously to those who wrote to her or told her how much it meant to them. Like much American poetry of the period, Dodge's serious verse was earnest, elevated, reassuring, and consolatory. But like much commonplace poetry of the time, it aimed only at being "quiet and unambitious, like a pleasant thought when such are wanted, sweet and chaste in moral influence."[6]

Unlike other women poets of the era, Dodge was not a poet of exaggerated sensibility. She was detached, reserved, protective of her own emotional privacy. Dodge's "serious" poetry attempts to come to terms with various challenges to individual human happiness: the passage of time; the separation from loved ones brought about by death; religious uncertainties; questions about the appropriate attitude toward nature's apparent cruelty or indifference. Her poems seem designed to serve the reader by expressing the sort of thoughts an average person might share. They are neither deep nor learned; nor are they especially original in thought or expression. A modest gracefulness of expression is their greatest charm. Sometimes they are prosaic; occasionally, banal or clichéd. But they are dignified and sincere, and apparently were enjoyed for the way they expressed what many people felt but perhaps could not readily put into words, and for their gentle optimism and reassurance.

Dodge confronted the realities of death and human limitation in her poems but refused to be gloomy or lachrymose. Her poetry is full of strategies for dealing with desolation of feeling, or despair at some great and irreversible loss. The responses she proposes to such enormous blows vary. The most common solution is the simple expedient of taking a larger view, since life may not be as it seems to those of a limited perspective. In "Inverted," for example, she suggests that though the common wisdom is otherwise, perhaps youth is more a time of keen disappointment than age is, for the latter may turn out to have its "pleasures, rosy fresh and warm" as well as its own "glad beguilements and expectancies" (*AW*, 14).

A few of Dodge's poems deal with the impact on the living of the death of a loved one. in "From Flower to Light" she suggests that an individual's loss can be accepted if the loved one is seen as transfigured, just as the colors of the lost flowers of summer are repeated in the heightened color of the leaves in autumn or the ordinary day is made lovely by the glow of the sunset as night comes on (*AW*, 42–45). "The Child and the Sea" suggests that the nature that can appear cruel or indifferent has been created by a God who "loveth every soul" and therefore there is no need for despair (*AW*, 46–47). In "The Master Hand" life is seen as a painting by a superb artist. This poem attempts to make sense of loss and diminishment by seeing them as necessary to a divine plan. Those lines which represent the speaker's life may be "obscure and gray and drear," but, says the speaker, "His picture was in need of me, / And he hath set me here" (*PV*, 49–50).

Most of these poems imply that the adoption of the right attitude toward pain and suffering can offer comfort, consolation, and resolution of conflict. Yet it is hard not to feel that the resolutions presented are more asserted than achieved. Occasionally the verses themselves suggest something of the real impatience or reluctance to accept things the way they are that still remains with the speaker, despite a strong effort of will to adopt a positive view. The coming of the night, for example, in "From Flower to Light" brings an end to the modest comfort the speaker has gleaned from her efforts to think her way out of her grief. She looks at the skies in the West, transfigured and glorious, until "the gates of the sunset, slow folding / Shut them out from . . . [her] passionate sight." But nothing in the poem suggests that the night that follows is any the brighter for the sunset (*AW*, 42–45).

Dodge's own doubts about her ability to respond to nature comprehensively, as the sort of poet she considered "great" did, are suggested in her meditative "By the Lake." "Nature's deep lessons come in silences, / Or sounds that fall like silence on our sense," and so the "plashing" of the water seems to ask her probing questions about her "soul's pretense" and to expose "to searching light its fond alliances." But the speaker cannot fathom what her soul hides "nor sound the centres that the waves conceal." Though she may not be a poetic seer, she has sufficient sensibility to feel "The urging of the low, insistent tide,—/ Till the plashing seems like sobbing, and the sky grows cold and wide" (AW, 36–37).

Perhaps it was Dodge's doubt abut the merit of her own poetry that prompted her to title her collected poems rather modestly. She named one book *Poems and Verses* (but didn't say which were which). And she gave the other book the casual title *Along the Way*, adding this epigraph from Keats: "The Air that floated by me seemed to say: / 'Write'! / And so I did." The stress on spontaneity is perhaps a way of defusing the tension connected with presuming to be a poet, as well as—quite probably—an accurate description of the casual origin of a number of the pieces.

Verses, Rhymes, and Jingles

Much of Dodge's light verse for adults treats manners and social behavior that struck her as amusing. Many verses deal with the relationship between the sexes. She describes flirtation, courtship rituals, marriage proposals—all distanced by a humorous approach. The unspoken assumption of many of these poems is that young men and women leave their deepest feelings unadmitted and unspoken until circumstances surprise them into a recognition of their mutual affection. In "Snowbound" (PV, 105–6), "At the Picture Gallery" (PV, 98–99), and "A Monday Romance" (PV, 187–91) Dodge observes the game of flirtation as it was played in her day with a recognition of its absurdities and of the constraints it placed on women, who were conventionally cast in a passive role.

Sometimes Dodge spoke more directly of the frustrations and distortions custom could occasion in women's emotional lives. In "Miss Flip at the Exposition" (PV, 113–18) a scatterbrained young belle who gets very little out of a visit to the great Philadelphia Exposition reveals her own superficiality and silliness in her gushing conversation with a friend. But there are hints in some of her asides that she is playing a role dictated to her by the men in her life, whose approval means everything to her. Her frank interest in the dirty, busy workmen at the exposition is disapproved of by them and must be denied. And she wistfully talks of having seen so many people who are doing just what they want to do, something apparently out of the question for her. The hint is that, absurd as she is, she is this way because she is playing an acceptable but unnatural social role that requires she deny her real feelings.

Dodge wrote verses for children readily, often to fill some pressing editorial need. Some of her work is casual to the point of shapelessness—obvious filler that loses in an anthology whatever point it might once have had in the context of an illustration or the theme of a particular issue of *St. Nicholas* or *Hearth and Home*. But the most serious failing of the verses is their occasional sentimentality. When Dodge writes of children as objects of adult affection or when she writes for adults, evoking the charm of children and trying to tug the heartstrings, her tone becomes arch and the effect is cloying and self-indulgent.

The best of Dodge's poems for children are of two sorts. One is the very simple and neatly put didactic sentiment about nature, designed to encourage children to notice and appreciate what they see around them. The other is a kind of updated Mother Goose piece, with clever rhymes, amusing characters with odd-sounding names, and lots of amiable nonsense. As a children's poet, Dodge was certainly not in a league with Edward Lear, Lewis Carroll, or Christina Rossetti; her comic verse at its best was more like that of Laura E. Richards or Tudor Jenks. But Dodge's humor and good-natured sense of fun appealed to her child audience, who enjoyed her witty wordplay, her willingness to be silly, and (since the later poems were usually printed with their *St. Nicholas* illustrations) the often-delightfully-absurd combination of poem and picture she provided for them.

Dodge's poems for children reflect the same ethos as her fiction. Even her youngest readers are urged to accept the trials that come their way without self-pity and to be grateful for their blessings. In

"Resolution" they are urged to do, with firmness and initiative, what conscience tells them. Part of their responsibility seems to be to doubt any "hollow creed" no matter what others might say. The idea seems to be to follow one's inner light bravely, whether one's life be "bright or drear" (*RJ*, 262–63).

For Dodge, it is important to work or play wholeheartedly. Children are told to look at nature to see that constant labor is "the price of . . . thriving" (*RJ*, 29). And they are urged to play vigorously in winter, for "Fun is the fuel / For driving off cold" (*RJ*, 34). Above all, children in Dodge's nursery world are supposed to be— no matter what the provocation—glad, cheerful, and brave; whining and fretting are mortal sins in Dodge's nursery morality. Dodge seems to envision a family situation in which parents turn to children for hope and love and the courage to go on. Such an attitude puts emotional pressure on the child to provide a cheerful note in a sometimes-cheerless world. In "Hark! My Children" Dodge tells children to be like the stars, which, when it is dark, sparkle anyway; the leaves, which keep the flowers warm despite being tossed by storms; and the birds, who sing the gloom of the forest away (*RJ*, 235). Similarly, in "Fire Flies" gentle souls "glimmer and glow," "[t]eaching a lesson wherever they go" (*RJ*, 259–60).

Though Dodge's verses about children and parents are sometimes mawkishly emotional, she manages in one to keep a nice sense of detachment. "Taking Time to Grow" is a fable about children's desire for independence. Two eaglets whose father has told them of a wren who "flew about so brave and bold / When it was scarcely four weeks old" are eager to do likewise and see the world "so grand and gay." But their fiercely protective mother manages to say no without crushing their ambition. She tells them, "As for wrens—a wren's a wren," but "an eaglet can afford to wait" (*RJ*, 44–45).

Dodge's didactic impulse was sometimes blunted by her awareness of the pleasures of naughtiness. The primary appeal of her poem "Among the Animals" is the opportunity it gives for the child reader to empathize with the destructive impulse of a child who frankly enjoys breaking things, jumping and stamping on a new

Noah's Ark, and feeling "as grand as would be" until retribution strikes in the form of a parental spanking (*RJ*, 44–45).

Dodge often rings changes on traditional nursery lore, updating it for the late nineteenth century. A pert young lady—who probably reads *St. Nicholas* and is up on her astronomy—in the poem "Informed" muses:

> Twinkle, twinkle, little star—
> I don't wonder what you are!
> I've learned more of you, you see,
> Than you'll ever know of me. (*AW*, 121)

And in "Mother Goose for Big Folks" the nonsense world of nursery rhymes is wryly compared with the real world in which everyone cries for mother, eats and drinks too much, and foolishly does what makes least sense, so that the "gist of our lives from first to last, / Is under their jingle hid" (*PV*, 178–80).

Collections

Those verses Dodge wished to acknowledge and keep in print she collected in several volumes. In 1874 *Rhymes and Jingles*, a lively collection of early verse, mostly from her *Hearth and Home* days, was published. Critics described the volume as "full of queer, quaint fancies, abounding with humor, but without much sentiment or pathos,"[7] and as "full of comical wise nonsense and the most felicitous absurdities of language."[8] *Along the Way* (1879) included some previously published poems for adults, a few verses from *Rhymes and Jingles* Dodge thought would appeal to adults, and a number of poems published for the first time. The subject matter ranges from simple verses about snowflakes and domestic life to meditations on nature, death, and loss. In 1894 she published *When Life Is Young: A Collection of Verse for Boys and Girls*. Though a few of these verses are first published there, many of them had appeared in *St. Nicholas*, some unsigned, others written under various pen names, and still others signed MMD.

Besides a good deal of light, humorous verse for children, this collection includes one of Dodge's most popular poems, "The Minuet," about a grandmother who prefers the stately measures of long ago to "modern . . . rushing, whirling, bumping" (*AW*, 107–9), as well as Dodge's poem on the death of Hans Christian Andersen (*LY*, 182–83) and her verses for Fayal Clarke about *Alice in Wonderland*, "To W.F.C." (*LY*, 150). In 1904 she published *Poems and Verses* containing some new poems and some chosen by request from among her verses for children.

Edmund C. Stedman, a prominent establishment critic of the time (and an old friend of Dodge's from her Newark days) thought that many of the American women poets of the genteel tradition— people like Dodge's friends Celia Thaxter, Lucy Larcom, and Helen Hunt Jackson—were writing genuine poetry—not terribly original, and sometimes a bit thin, but spontaneous, artistic, knowledgeable, elevating, and pleasantly conventional. He called Dodge a natural singer in her way and said her stanzas were "marked by charming fancy and always tender and sweet." And, he added, she had "a gift" "of seeing into the hearts of children." Altogether, these modest compliments were probably a fair assessment of Dodge's poetic achievement. Her readers may have been a little more enthusiastic, however, for, young and old, they kept her collections of poetry profitably in print during her lifetime, and her best-known poems, "The Two Mysteries" and "The Minuet," remained popular anthology pieces for some time.

6

Donald and Dorothy

In *Donald and Dorothy* Dodge produced exactly the sort of story she liked to serialize in *St. Nicholas*. It had mystery and suspense to keep readers coming back month after month; a durable, sentimental romance plot; a quest; and enough amusing episodes and eccentric characters to please a wide range of readers. The novel appeared in *St. Nicholas* beginning with the first four chapters in December 1881 and concluding in the final issue of volume 9 in October 1882. A release of the book by November 1882, in time for Christmas sales, might have capitalized on the interest aroused during its serialization. But Dodge had for some time been eager to renegotiate her standing contracts with Charles Scribner and was determined to use *Donald and Dorothy* (which both she and Scribner thought might prove to be another property as lucrative as *Hans Brinker*) to gain leverage in these discussions. Dodge wanted a contract that would allow her the right to take her books—not only new ones but her earlier books as well—to another publisher after a few years. Understandably, Scribner could not see his way clear to offer Dodge the options she demanded, and he lost the book to Thomas Niles of Boston's Roberts Brothers, which had done so much for Louisa May Alcott. Dodge lost valuable time during these negotiations, however, and didn't actually have a contract until 19 July 1883 (Wright 1979, 130).

Critical Reception

To judge from the enthusiasm of writers to the "Letter-Box" department of the magazine, *Donald and Dorothy* was warmly received by its first readers. Nellie G. from Kentucky termed it "just splendid."[1] Daisy Brown of Chicago confessed that when called to supper while reading the September issue of *St. Nicholas*, she had sat on the magazine to make sure none of her brothers would get hold of it before she had finished. She said they were all "much interested" in the novel and were "sorry to have it end."[2]

Dorothy's picture was pronounced "perfectly lovely" by one reader,[3] and a boy from New Orleans was so taken with it that he wrote to ask whether Dorothy lived in New York, adding, "All the boys that I know, who have seen the engraving, have fallen dead in love with her, including myself." Dodge replied to his letter: "Dorothy's picture came to us all the way from England. It is an excellent likeness, however, and the original is living in———. But no; eighty thousand boys would be too many admirers, and if they all should try to call on New Year's Day, what would poor Dorothy do! Besides, E.T. [Ed Tyler, Dorothy's beau in the story] might object to our giving the address to so many boys."[4]

Though *Donald and Dorothy* never approached the popularity of *Hans Brinker*, it went quickly through one English and two American editions. And the Century Company generously allowed Roberts Brothers to use "all the illustrations used in *St. Nicholas*; 4000 copies of an edition of 5000 sold the first year, the 5th thousand by six months later" (Wright 1979, 130). The *Century* termed *Donald and Dorothy* a "novelette for young people, as it combines the complications and suspense of a definite plot with some charming pictures of home life," and remarked that "though ostensibly for young people, the story . . . is of a kind to interest children of a larger growth."[5] Dodge's colleague Fayal Clarke, who thought of *Donald and Dorothy* as "the narrative of a boy's chivalrous love for his sister," said it was one of Dodge's personal favorites among her books and recalled that at the height of its popularity a number of children were named after the hero and heroine. He singled out its "original and absorbing plot" and its "full share of the author's rich humor" as particular strengths (Clarke 1905, 1066).

Recent Criticism

Donald and Dorothy has not drawn a great deal of critical attention in recent years, and when it has been noticed by critics it has usually been compared—unfavorably—with *Hans Brinker*. Catharine Morris Wright considered it to be charming and apropos for *St. Nicholas* but felt it "had none of the fire and directness, the adventure and spirit of *Hans*." The novel, she said, was "calculated to entrance its readers with an obvious but baffling mystery" (Wright 1979, 125) but would disappoint anyone looking for something like *Hans Brinker*: it was "ordinary, unremarkable, everyday" (Wright 1979, 130).

Interesting parallels between Alcott's *Eight Cousins* (which had run in *St. Nicholas* in 1875) were pointed out by Marilyn Karrenbrock in her article on Dodge in the *Dictionary of Literary Biography*. But for Karrenbrock, there are problems, too: the portrayal of Donald and Dorothy's attachment to each other is "excessively sentimental," and though the mystery is "well plotted" the book "falls far behind *Hans Brinker*" (Karrenbrock, 42:157). Harriet Christy was more positive, saying that the "charm pervading this story for nineteenth-century readers was not only its mystery and suspense but also its domestic setting," though she noted such shortcomings as lack of character development and imagery, and an unsophisticated style (Christy, 198).

Plot and Structure

Striking similarities exist in the central situations explored in *Hans Brinker* and *Donald and Dorothy*. In each book a disturbance in the relationship between a father and a daughter must be corrected before the central difficulties of the plot can be resolved. The failure of their parents' generation to investigate a disastrous set of events and to deal effectively with its results threatens a young brother and sister. The girl is in each case in more danger: she is faced with loss of caste and a life of drudgery, and even her physical safety is put at risk by the failures of her elders.

The plot of *Donald and Dorothy* turns on the question of Dorothy's true identity: is she Dorothy Reed or Delia Robertson? When the story opens, three babies—Donald Reed, his sister Dorothy, and their cousin Delia—have been lost at sea. Donald and one little girl are saved, but which girl? The two are brought up as brother and sister. But 14 years after the shipwreck, a question is raised about the girl's identity. Donald and the girl he knows as Dorothy are either twins or cousins. She is the ward either of George Reed, whom she has learned to love, or of a sinister stranger named Eben Slade. If she is Dorothy Reed, she has the right to remain in the comfortable, secure home in which she has grown up; if she is Delia Robertson, she faces an uncertain future of drudgery on the frontier, in the home of Slade and the wife he claims to have left behind, "somewhere" in the West (*DD*, 87).

The story begins slowly, and only gradually is the fact that a question has been raised about Dorothy's identity made clear to readers. Dodge teases her audience with references to a dark man lurking in the shrubbery of the Reed estate, and Uncle George, a pleasant but remote father figure, grows moody and tense. Once the dark stranger, Eben Slade, has forced George's hand, Dorothy must be told that her identity is in question. At this point, Donald's and George's fears are realized: Dorothy decides that she will do her duty to her real family when the truth about her identity is determined, even if doing so means a life as Slade's ward. George Reed is paralyzed by fear and guilt, for his sister Kate had consigned her daughter to Slade's care only because she thought George and her adoptive family had abandoned her. But Donald, though only 15, boldly volunteers to travel to Europe in order to search for evidence of Dorothy's real identity.

As the *Century* pointed out, *Donald and Dorothy* is basically a romance, and it is unthinkable that it should end unhappily. Like much nineteenth-century melodrama, it depicts "transgressions against the happiness and respectability of the middle-class family structure" that "inevitably" lead to defeat for the transgressor.[6] Moral concern is aroused in behalf of the Reeds, characters representing traditional middle-class domestic values—family honor, honesty, financial responsibility—and fortune operates to support those values as the required happy ending unfolds.

In choosing a plot of this nature Dodge was working with familiar formulas of nineteenth-century fiction: the figures of the pampered heiress who becomes poor in midadolescence but meets the challenge nobly[7] and the young man who must undertake the traditional romantic quest for his true identity, his inheritance, and all that brings fullness of life. Earlier in the century the audience for women's fiction had responded enthusiastically to sentimental stories of female heroism, but after the Civil War novels of this strain began to be published largely in the form of didactic fiction for young girls (Baym, 296–98). The adult reading public showed at this time a new interest in gothic romances and a readiness to "appreciate a more androgynous literature" (Baym, 298) depicting men and women with common social and religious interests.

In *Donald and Dorothy* Dodge combines the female heroism plot with the male-oriented adventure plot and adds touches of mystery and romance. She retains the moral earnestness of much earlier fiction and its vision of home as a world of personal relations and affections, a kind of moral bastion against a dangerous and corrupt world. Her twin protagonists—the disciplined, selfless brother and the reckless, impetuous sister who keep asserting their essential oneness—were designed to appeal to a primary audience of young people of both sexes.

Donald sees the questioning of Dorothy's identity as a questioning of his own identity and his position in the world: "If she was not Dorry, then who was he? Who was uncle George? Who were all the persons they knew, and what did everything in life mean?" (*DD*, 258). His story depicts a series of educative and testing experiences that prepare him for the tasks ahead. Donald's triumphs are clear-cut, external events: he saves his sister from a runaway horse and from a mad dog; he investigates a cold trail of clues in foreign countries where he barely speaks the language, yet comes home with definitive proof that Dorothy is his twin sister. Dorothy by contrast, never leaves home, never undertakes a grand quest; however, she is given an opportunity to "transcend the perils of plot with a self-exalting dignity."[8] When Dorothy faces the possible loss of all that has given her social identity, she finds the strength to define herself in her own terms. Paradoxically, the parents who have previously been but shadowy figures to her now become much more distinct and real as she prays for the "strength to do what was right—even to go with Eben Slade to his distant home, *if she were really his sister's child!*" (*DD*, 284). In her decision to do her duty as Delia Robertson, if that is who she is, Dorothy achieves a kind of moral triumph, an inner victory of the sort sentimental heroines in the nineteenth-century novel were customarily allowed.

Narrative Technique

Hans Brinker begins with an engaging skating scene; *Donald and Dorothy*, with a daring but awkwardly executed narrative maneuver—a brief chapter, "In Which None of the Characters Appear," that functions rather like the scenes that run in modern films during the credits. In this chapter the news of the shipwreck from which Donald and Dorothy have been saved arrives at the Reed estate, but Dodge withholds the nature of the disaster from her readers. The only clue is to be found in a tiny illustration of a foundering ship worked into an "illuminated" letter in the first sentence. The story of the shipwreck is, however, told and retold during the novel, and each time, what actually happened becomes clearer. These retellings structure the narrative, directing readers' attention to the way the pieces of the puzzle are being put together, reviewing the essentials of a complicated plot, and heightening suspense. Once the full story of the shipwreck has been revealed, Dodge closes with a short final chapter, which, like the first, is entirely without dialogue. The novel ends with a *tableau vivant*: a radiant Donald and Dorothy step out of their carriage "happiest of the happy" (*DD*, 355).

Donald and Dorothy uses not only a highly formulaic mystery story of a kind very popular in the nineteenth century—a familiar romance plot capable of engaging a popular audience—but a variety of set pieces that Dodge knew from experience she could do well. Dodge's strong management of the reader-narrator relationship allows her to include, without losing her readers' attention, long interpolated episodes that do not seem to develop the plot. Many of these episodes describe the pleasures and amusements of a country summer. These interludes increase suspense and are designed to have a special appeal to a young audience. They often involve play, games, contests, and exciting or dangerous events. Some of them echo essential elements of the mystery plot, offering patterns of action involving threat, risk, and rescue. And occasionally an episode seems to exist in order to make emotionally available to younger readers some aspect of a scene, characterization, or relationship that would not be within their ordinary range of experience.

The threat represented by Eben Slade, for example, is easily understood by younger readers as the stealing away of a young girl from her family. But the darker hints about Slade—that he is no gentleman, that he is perhaps a criminal, and that he is possibly a sexual threat to Dorothy—are conveyed most effectively in the sequence in which the brother and sister are forced to stop at a sleazy hotel when Dorothy's pony goes lame. The atmosphere is oppressive, sinister. Slade here is in his element and is bold, insinuating, and more offensive than he can ever be at the Reed estate. Dorothy's flight from the hotel is a hair's-breadth escape from all that Eben Slade represents for her future. Donald's quick action here saves his sister from an ugly confrontation, just as elsewhere in the novel he saves her from physical danger.

Many of the interpolated episodes describe an educational regime of study, exercise, play, and social activity similar to that which Dodge encouraged in the pages of *St. Nicholas*. Donald and his friends build a gym; Dorothy organizes a Girls' Botany Club; and both boys and girls fence and ride. There is a shooting match at which the boys compete, the girls serving as the admiring (though distracting) audience. But when the boys decide to exploit the girls' sympathy by staging a fake accident during a boat race, Dorothy sees through the plan and arranges to have the "audience" slip quietly away, leaving the boys to perform to an empty lakeshore. This cool, unsentimental response to a mock "shipwreck" stands in interesting contrast to the rapt attention given the many retellings of the story of the wreck from which the twins have originally been saved.

Inspired perhaps by Lucretia Hale's popular stories about the Peterkin family, Dodge gave the Reeds a family called Danby as neighbors. Mr. and Mrs. Danby are a good-hearted couple whose 12 children provide comic relief and serve as objects of the Reeds' enlightened charity. Ben Buster, the eldest son, has seen more of the world than Donald and Dorothy but is uneasily aware that his little brothers and sisters, under the good influence of the Reeds, have, during his absence, acquired smoother manners and higher aspirations than he possesses. Dorothy, like Hilda in *Hans Brinker*, has been an enabling figure, insisting that Charity Cora be allowed to join the Botany Club, and helping with her schoolwork. Charity's older sister, Amanda, is the subject of much teasing because of her constant writing of verse and her passion to "perfect herself," but by the end of the story she wins the opportunity to go away to school and become a teacher. Younger readers may especially enjoy the pranks of young Fandy Danby, who invents wild games, insists on "fencing" with Donald, and preaches to his assembled brothers and sisters a sermon that is a wry comment on heavy-handed adult didacticism.

The Danbys figure in a long set piece describing an elaborate house picnic that goes on for 10 hours. Dodge thought well enough of this segment of the novel to let it stand alone in one issue of *St. Nicholas* when the story was serialized—despite her usual concern about teasing readers along with suspenseful plot twists. The house picnic is one of Dodge's specialties, the description of an elaborate, festive gathering that works to release the energies and talents of hosts and guest alike. The guests take over the Reed mansion from piazza to attic, and there is an activity for everyone, from the taffy pull in the kitchen to parlor games of the sort Dodge had described in *A Few Friends*.

Some of the events at the party pick up the thematics of the story. While Amanda spends her day quietly "perfecting herself" in the library, her little brother improvises a hunting game reminiscent of the many ritualized combats in the story. The concern of the mystery plot with portraits, photographs, role-playing, and identity emerges in some of the party games, and the exchange of mottoes and gifts at the end of the day previews what happens at the end of the novel, when baby clothes, locket, key, photographs, and other documents must find their way into the proper hands. Though the novel's plot does not seem to be advanced by the account of the party, the life-enhancing activities going on there reveal a rich cultural and social environment, satisfying affective relationships of many sorts, security, and comfort—all that Dorothy would lose in leaving her home.

Gender Roles

Much has been said of the cult of "True Womanhood" in the nineteenth century, the code by which American women were judged by their "piety, purity, submissiveness and domesticity."[9] In its extreme form this standard exalted meek passivity, dependence, and a strong sense of inferiority among young women. But feminists were not alone in taking exception to this view of the female role. By the 1860s, certainly many "middle of the road" people of both sexes were coming to admire the woman of "intelligence, physical fitness and health, self sufficiency, [and] economic self reliance."[10] Many of those who wished women to be actively fit, intelligent, and self-sufficient did not see themselves as doing more than modestly expanding the scope of feminine abilities and responsibilities. Yet despite their traditional rhetoric, such views constituted a challenge to the conservative vision of a thoroughly subordinated women—something Dodge herself seems never to have been.

In *Donald and Dorothy* Dodge endows her heroine with a number of spirited, even aggressive qualities. Dorothy is a risk taker who enjoys riding fast horses, and she speaks her mind more freely than her brother. She says early in the story that she is glad her brother is her twin "because twins can't boss—I mean domineer—each other. If Don was the least bit older than me— I—me, it wouldn't be half so nice as starting fair and square." Her uncle George, ever wrongheaded, responds to this speech by withdrawing his arm from around her shoulders and warning her to stop her nonsense (*DD*, 33). A moment later he is calling her Donald's "little sister," though Dodge makes it clear that Dorothy looks older than her brother (*DD*, 35).

Over and over in the story we hear Dorothy demanding the truth, asking why. When her uncle tells the young people to avoid Eben Slade, she wants to know the reason; Donald at this point is shown as either less curious or more discreet. George's conversation in this scene is described metaphorically as a "deep stream passing between two banks—one [Dorothy] with its sunny leaves and blossoms all astir in the breeze, the other [Donald] bending, casting its image in the stream, and so going on with it in a closer companionship" (*DD*, 35). Donald is in many ways like his uncle, especially in his willingness to keep Dorothy in the dark for her own good. When Dorothy impetuously questions her uncle about Slade, George breaks in on her with a firm "You need not see nor try to see. Only remember what I have told you" (*DD*, 37).

Though in one sense the mystery plot is resolved happily through Donald's efforts, asserting "rational order over secrecy, chaos and irrationality," and his adventure story appears to "play out the fantasy of heroic triumph over insuperable obstacles" (Cawelti, 45), the story also embodies a protest against the masculine control and domination of women by showing such behavior in a negative light. If Uncle George is the model patriarch, he is also a neurotic, troubled figure, unequal to the task of protecting his niece largely because of unresolved conflicts over his own behavior toward the Aunt Kate of whom Dorothy so powerfully reminds him. When Donald, whose comradely acceptance that they are equals has meant so much to her, enters into his uncle's plan to protect Dorothy from the truth, young readers are invited to experience the pain and tension of the situation from Dorothy's point of view.

And when Donald does manage to solve the mystery, it is only because he is able to engage the sympathy and help of two women and to develop in himself strengths often associated in the late nineteenth century with the female role. The first of the women who helps him is a housewife who gave a dress to the twins' nursemaid, Ellen Lee, when she was rescued from the shipwreck. Donald rummages through her family scrap bag and finds a piece of Ellen's black dress. Ellen, who, fearing she has been the cause of the twins' death, has deliberately avoided being found, later proves her identity by producing from her own scrap bag a matching piece of that black dress. Donald's real strength proves to be not his marksmanship or his physical courage but his ability to establish rapport with these women: his willingness to pore over baby photos and baby clothes with them, to learn to tell one kind of dress material from another, to be patient, to empathize, to listen.

When George and Donald refuse to tell Dorothy about Slade, they do their best to prevent her from encountering a real challenge, which she needs in order to come to full maturity. The patriarchal view that women have a separate sphere of life from men is invoked to protect Dorothy from acting on the principles her uncle and brother claim to revere in her. By lying to her, they situate her in a pastoral prison they have created out of their need to defend against the forces of personal and social chaos represented by the have-not Eben Slade.

Images of enclosure, confinement, and imprisonment abound in the novel. Dorothy is confined to the Reed estate, behind iron gates and locked doors, and her brother is admonished to guard her at all times. Even as a baby, she is singled out by her mother to be given the locket with key and triple chain that ultimately helps solve the mystery of her identity. (The cover of one edition of the novel even featured an embossed chain decoration, pointing up the importance to the whole book of the image of the chain that grew too tight for Dorothy's neck.)[11]

Projected in much of Dodge's work is a deep uneasiness about the unfairness of a world in which some people are happy, safe, healthy, and rich while others are ill, wretched, and struggling to make ends meet. A life with Slade would expose Dorothy to real dangers for which her sheltered life has not prepared her. But by facing up to the worst that could happen, Dorothy has a chance to discover who she truly is—when not defined by her family, her position in society, or her possessions. Strangely enough, she is never freer than when she is most threatened, for the happy ending that establishes her social identity robs her of her autonomy: once there is no doubt that she *is* Dorothy Reed, the shades of the prison house begin to close about her.

Thus, the book's requirements for a conventional happy ending appear also to require that Dodge's lively heroine subside into meek domesticity. Although earlier in the novel Donald gives up the chance of going away to school so as to stay with his sister, at the novel's close he gets to go happily off to Columbia College. Dorothy—who has been his superior in history, botany, and rhetoric—must stay at home, struggling (not too successfully) to learn to bake cakes and bread and to iron shirts because her Uncle George thinks "every lady should understand housekeeping" (*DD*, 265). Dodge herself believed that a knowledge of housekeeping was something every woman should posses, but she also believed that young girls should be prepared for a larger sphere of interest. (As noted earlier, she was instrumental in Annie Nathan Meyer's efforts to persuade the academic establishment at Columbia to create Barnard College for women.) And it is interesting to note that two of the women who face financially uncertain futures at the end of *Donald and Dorothy* look forward eagerly to careers (Amanda Danby is preparing to "perfect herself" as a teacher, and Ellen Lee hopes to establish herself as a dressmaker), whereas for Dorothy the confirmation that she is destined to enjoy inherited wealth and position means the end of her formal education.

There is evidence that Dodge's readers, and perhaps the author herself, sensed an unresolved tension in the ending of *Donald and Dorothy*. It is clear from the "Letter-Box" responses that many readers hated to see the serialization end. And Dodge herself told Thomas Niles of Roberts Brothers that she hoped to be able to insert "a whole new chapter at the close in consequence of the request of (literally) hundreds of boys and girls, and because I thought such an addition if announced, would help the sale of the book very materially." But she fell ill while preparing the book for the press, and her illness "defeated the plan," since she couldn't "write the chapter hurriedly" and did not want to "mar the artistic structure of the story."[12] Perhaps she regretted the decision not to write the chapter, for three years later she wistfully confided to Niles that letters were still coming to her from children, begging for a sequel.[13]

The adults who expected from the author of *Hans Brinker* and the editor of *St. Nicholas* a wholesome, edifying book for young people no doubt found what they wanted in *Donald and Dorothy*; the rather idealized brother and sister whose story it is would have seemed model children—brave, reverent, dutiful, clean, and "true." But like *Hans*, this novel dramatized the tensions between the generations and offered an implicit critique of some of the social values it appeared to support, particularly as they concerned the upbringing of young girls. Although Dodge's novels appear to preach self-sacrifice, discipline, and respect for one's elders, they are not uncritical of the status quo, and their sympathy for young people's need to assume responsibility for their own lives endeared them to their young readers.

7

The Conductor of *St. Nicholas*

Mary Mapes Dodge's most enduring contribution to American literature was her editorial work for *St. Nicholas* magazine from 1873 to 1905. This chapter centers on Dodge as editor, setting her work in the context of the cultural mission undertaken by her publisher, Scribner and Company, and considering her relationships with her editorial staff and her double audience of parents and children. The next chapter will examine her work with contributors, drawing on Dodge's correspondence, the archives of her publishers, and a comparative study of manuscripts and published texts, for though Dodge did not publish any extended account of her editorial philosophy, there is much to be learned about her aims and methods through a close scrutiny of such sources.

Scribner and Company

Dodge's publishers were committed to commercial success but also had a strong social agenda. Charles Scribner, Roswell Smith, and Josiah Holland addressed themselves to an audience that was conservative in its moral views, high-minded, and committed to such traditional values as patriotism, respect for the family, hard work, self-reliance, and social concern. Scribner and Company had come into existence in 1869, when Holland and Smith persuaded publisher Charles Scribner to launch a new magazine in New York to compete with *Harper's Monthly* and Boston's prestigious and popular *Atlantic Monthly*. The new magazine was a lively, cosmopolitan journal appealing to the same readership as its rivals, yet it was marked with Holland's concern for high moral standards. Holland was its editor, assisted by Dodge's old friend Richard Watson Gilder. In 1870 they introduced *Scribner's Monthly* with a commitment to providing "the best reading that money could buy," "the finest illustrations procurable at home and abroad," a "magazine . . . as good as we can make it" with "something in every number that will interest and instruct every member of every family into which it shall have the good fortune to find its way."[1]

The 1870s were a difficult time in the United States. The Civil War was over, but the North and the South had not yet really come together. "A new industrial order was transforming an agrarian nation, threatening old individualistic values, creating new wealth that bred corruption in both business and government as well as new pockets of poverty that poisoned the growing cities." Urban areas were faced with the need to assimilate large numbers of immigrants. Panic and depression undermined confidence in the country's financial stability, and "the religion that, diverse as it was, had provided the basis for cultural unity, was under challenge."[2]

The editors of the new magazine, *Scribner's Monthly*, aimed high, hoping to "heal the estrangement of religion and science" and to "bridge the gap between culture and the common people" (Chew, 77). Holland and Gilder hoped that "the American middle class, if sufficiently exposed to the traditional culture and traditional values" espoused by Scribner and Company, "would move to a higher plane of appreciation for literature and art, would impose morality on American public life, and would create a just, ordered, and gracious society" (John, ix).

Scribner's Monthly was a miscellany designed to appeal to open-minded, upper-middle-class readers who saw themselves as leaders whose tastes and attitudes were worthy of emulation by others, a group especially eager to pass on its values—and the social status associated with them—to its children. Within a few years the new magazine's circulation reached 100,000. But as the editors constantly advised their readers to share the magazine with others in order to diffuse its cultural message more widely, the real readership, it has been estimated, was probably closer to a half-million (Chew, 77). To serve their family audience more completely, Smith, Holland, and Scribner decided in 1873 to extend their efforts to the publishing of a children's magazine that would be welcomed in every home that took *Scribner's Monthly.*

Dodge described in an interview what happened when she received Smith's request for a letter "embodying her idea of a magazine for children." Apparently, "in the writing the letter developed into an article," and so, Dodge said, she drew her pen through the heading "and sent with the manuscript a note asking Mr. Roswell Smith to let me have it again" to publish in *Hearth and Home.*[3] But Smith kept the piece, paid her, and published it in *Scribner's Monthly* instead. The essay has acquired justifiable fame as the statement of principles on which *St. Nicholas* was founded.

"The child's magazine," Dodge asserted, "must not be a milk-and-water variety of the adult's periodical." In fact, it "needs to be stronger, truer, bolder, more uncompromising than the other." It should be full of "cheer," "freshness," "heartiness," "life and joy" ("CM," 352). "Therefore," she said, "look to it that it be strong, warm, beautiful and true." Above all, she maintained, the magazine must be designed to please as well as instruct its readers:

> Most children of the present civilization attend school. Their little heads are strained and taxed with the day's lessons. They do not want to be bothered nor amused nor taught not petted. They just want to have their own way over their own magazine. They want to enter the one place where they may come and go as they please, where they are not obliged to mind, or say "yes, ma'm" and "yes, sir,"—where, in short, they can live a brand-new, free life of their own for a little while, accepting acquaintances as they choose and turning their backs without ceremony upon what does not concern them. ("CM," 353)

Though she felt it needed to be entertaining, fresh, and natural, Dodge also believed the child's periodical had a moral mission, which was to be carried out unobtrusively "by hints dropped incidentally here and there; by a few brisk, hearty statements of the difference between right and wrong; a sharp clean thrust at falsehood, a sunny recognition of truth, a gracious application of politeness, an unwilling glimpse of the odious doings of the uncharitable and base" ("CM," 354).

Founding of *St. Nicholas*

Smith and Holland proposed that Dodge edit a new magazine for them, based on the plan she had outlined in her article. Thus, in March 1873 she left *Hearth and Home* to work for Scribner and Company. To a large extent, Dodge shared her publishers' morality, taste, and strong sense of cultural mission. Her journal was designed to do its part in teaching its young readers "how to live," fostering in them a love of hard work as well as "courage, fortitude, self respect, and the golden rule." This program reflected traditional establishment values, but Dodge, like her associates in Scribner and Company, also put great stress on open-mindedness and an orientation to the future. *St. Nicholas* was to be fun, it was to build character, but it was also to keep "pace with the world and the important things that are going forward in it" and to prepare "boys and girls for life as it is."[4]

Despite the Panic of 1873, Scribner and Company was determined to launch the new magazine in style, with a solid advertising campaign that included strong support from *St. Nicholas*'s sister journal. A notice in the November 1873 *Scribner's Monthly* observed of the new magazine, "Whether we shall lead the little child, or the little child shall lead us, remains to be seen; but it will be pleasant to have him at our side, to watch his growth and development, and to minister, as we may, to his prosperity. . . . Wherever 'SCRIBNER' goes, 'ST. NICHOLAS' ought to go. They will be harmonious companions in the family, and the helpers of each other in the work of instruction, culture and entertainment" (Erisman, 378).

The response to *St. Nicholas* from young readers, parents, and critics was enthusiastic. In its advertising *St. Nicholas* triumphantly cited its glowing press notices. It was termed "the ideal of a children's magazine" and was said to have reached "the minds and hearts of the children as no other work, not even 'Our Young Folks,' " ever had.[5] The religious press as well as the secular press hailed Dodge for creating "for girls and boys a magazine . . . full of interest and brightness, its articles possessing much common sense and giving some instruction, evincing a fresh, simple and genuine spirit, and always looking toward what was good and beautiful and true," a magazine that could "be an actual instrument for developing the child's best and highest nature, and yet should never be stilted, priggish, or pietistic."[6]

And critics noted the success with which Dodge had managed to attract well-known authors for adults and to teach them how to address a younger audience:

> It is not often that so much ability and literary practice are combined in the conduct of a juvenile magazine. Almost every page bears the marks not only of talent, but tact,—a feature in which so many writers for children are wofully [sic] deficient. No one would anticipate that men like Bryant, Ik Marvel, Bret Harte, Charles Dudley Warner, C. P. Cranch, Clarence Cook, John Hay, and T. W. Higginson had any special gift for the delectation of the "youthful mind," but judging from their contributions in this volume they are "to the manner born," and find themselves no less at home in the nursery than in the arena of politics and in the higher walks of literature.[7]

Scribner and Company was quick to make use of testimonials from such figures as John Greenleaf Whittier and Charles Dudley Warner in its advertising for *St. Nicholas*. Whittier declared that "it is little to say of this magazine that it is the best child's periodical in the world, and I think the editor has great reason to congratulate herself upon it."[8] Warner concurred, adding that the magazine not only was the best magazine for children he'd ever seen but also was "even more entertaining for grown people than some of the quarterlies." He knew Dodge's aims and hopes for *St. Nicholas*: "the high ideal" she had for it "and her desire that it should exert a sweet and ennobling influence in the households of the land." After reading the first bound volume of the magazine, he concluded, "It has been made level with the comprehension of children, and yet it is a continual educator of their taste, and of their honor and courage. I do not see how it can be made any better, and if the children don't like it, I think it is time to begin to change the kind of children in this country."[9]

Scribner and Company had shrewdly bought out its most likely competitor in the children's field, Horace Scudder's *Riverside Magazine*, and in short succession managed to absorb (with its subscription lists) such journals as *Our Young Folks* and *Children's Hour* in 1874, *Schoolday Magazine* and *Little Corporal* in 1875, and *Wide Awake* in 1893. The magazine was well advertised and aggressively merchandised. In the early years, door-to-door canvassers and premium offers helped to swell sales and *St. Nicholas* soon established a circulation of 70,000 issues a month (Erisman, 378), with special holiday issues reaching an even higher circulation. This wide circulation is especially notable because the magazine, by the standards of the day, was not inexpensive, selling for 25¢ an issue, with a year's subscription for $3.00. Many bookstores sold individual issues, especially the holiday numbers, and the elaborate annual bound copies that were popular as gifts could cost up to $5.00, depending on their binding.

Despite the economic troubles of the time, *St. Nicholas* was not only a critical but a financial success, and its publishers were quick to give Dodge full credit for this achievement. After three short years, when *St. Nicholas* was well launched, Roswell Smith wrote a letter to Dodge summing up the way her publishers felt about her and what she had accomplished in that short time:

> I have said . . . that you were our choice as Editor of St. Nicholas, from all the world on either side of the ocean, so far as we knew it or could learn it. That you were left free to select your own assistants & to make so far as is

possible an ideal Periodical for children—and that your fitness for the position, your courage, industry, perseverance and resources had more than met our expectations and today it occurred to me that it might be pleasant to have me say just that to you. These are honest (not idle) words and I am sure they represent the sentiments of all my associates as well as myself.[10]

How did Dodge manage to achieve such a triumphant success so quickly and to maintain the excellence of St. Nicholas throughout her tenure as editor? An answer to this question can be found in the relationships Dodge was able to establish with her editorial staff, with her double audience of parents and children, and with her contributors.

Dodge and Her Staff

From the very beginning, Dodge's publishers relied on her judgment, answering any request for suggestions with "one unvarying answer: 'It is your magazine; do what you think best.' "[11] One of the first questions Dodge had to settle was the choice of a name for the new magazine, a choice that, she said in an interview, began to assume "gigantic proportions": "I wrote to two or three friends asking for suggestions, but none that were offered fulfilled what seemed to me an essential—that the name should belong to no time or nationality, and that it should belong inalienably to all children. I was in my aunt's drawing room one day, waiting for her return home, when I said to myself, 'You must find a name before you leave this room.' And then 'St. Nicholas' came to me. I never had a misgiving about it; it seemed impossible that I should ever have thought of any other."[12]

Dodge's work style reflected her training in journalism at Mapleridge. She chose her staff carefully and placed absolute confidence in them. The editorial staff was very much a family, and the editorial rooms under her direction took on the atmosphere of a home. Dodge was fortunate to be able to bring Frank Stockton along from *Hearth and Home* as associate editor of *St. Nicholas.* She trusted Stockton implicitly, and they shared similar views about what *St. Nicholas* needed. Stockton was an ingenious, talented writer on whom Dodge could depend for some of the best serial fiction *St. Nicholas* ever ran; he was also a hardworking editor who could run a busy office and was willing to pitch in and write appealing "filler" when material was scarce and deadlines loomed. Dodge relied on Stockton to run the editorial office in her absence. He held the fort during her visit to England in 1873 and, after he had left *St. Nicholas*, came back to fill in for Dodge when she had to be away for a few months on a trip to California. During the latter period he helped train young William Fayal Clarke to take his place as Dodge's right-hand man in the office, a post Clarke handled ably until Dodge's death.

Both Stockton and Clarke were congenial colleagues for Dodge, persons who "shared her own enthusiasm for the magazine and its readers" so that "the work was never drudgery to her nor to them." Clarke gave Dodge much of the credit for setting the tone of the office: "Her ardent zeal, keen wit, and tireless invention brightened with zest the dullest hour and the hardest task. Winter or summer, her spirits were unflagging, her powers always mettlesome and ready. Her mind teemed with ideas" (Clarke 1905, 1064).

Some commentators have noted that Dodge, during much of her career, came in to the office once a week, leaving the day-to-day-management of affairs to Clarke, Stockton, Tudor Jenks, and others. And they have assumed that this practice meant she kept a loose hand on the tiller. But Dodge was a strong editor, exercising close control over every aspect of her magazine, from designing the original cover (with her cousin Gus Wetmore), to supervising the layout, to negotiating with writers and artists, to planning each issue's and volume's contents in detail.

A careful reading of Dodge's literary correspondence and the letters and comments of those who worked for her suggests that though she put in relatively short hours at her office, she did a great deal of work at home. And it is clear from many memos— initialed by Dodge with brief cover notations—that it was common

practice for much manuscript material and editorial correspondence to come first to Dodge for an opinion. Then she would send
the item on with directions for some action by her assistants.
Dodge's correspondence with contributors, publishers, and readers was a constant and heavy responsibility. In an age in which
many people felt that receiving anything but a personally hand-
written message on an important matter was an insult, it was the
custom for editors to conduct their business correspondence in
longhand, a time-consuming task that Dodge could do as well at
home as in the office.

Dodge brought home what she termed her various "budgets" of
work to be dealt with. Letters to colleagues speak of her "immediate" budget of priority items and indicate that she worked on her
own time—often at odd hours and on Saturdays[13]—when she was
away from home on trips,[14] as well as when she was in New York.
She admitted to the "bad habit of writing without stay or pause
when . . . in the fervor of composition, and an utter inability to
work by the clock" (Tutwiler, 267–68). It was not uncommon for
messengers to bring manuscripts and other important papers to
her apartment in midtown Manhattan during the week, and sometimes other members of the staff would stop in to talk and have
lunch with Dodge. She had a home office, and sometimes a secre-
tary would work with her there. Of course, during much of the
time she edited *St. Nicholas* she had the advantage of having
Fayal Clarke at hand, for her assistant lived for some years as a
member of her own family, and later took an apartment not far
from her. And he was a frequent visitor to Yarrow, Dodge's summer hideaway at Onteora in the Catskills. It was only gradually,
during the last years of her life, that Clarke and his staff began
to assume a larger share of the editorial burden.

Dodge and Her Audience

By the time she became editor of *St. Nicholas*, Dodge's public
image was that of an accomplished writer with a special, rather
maternal interest in the welfare of young readers and the ability

to speak to them in a direct, fresh, realistic way. During the decades to come, she polished and perfected this image. The "Conductor" of *St. Nicholas* became a literary celebrity beloved by her young readers and seen by parents as a figure of authority whom they could trust to guide their children's reading.

A mere program—no matter how cleverly devised or well intentioned—is not sufficient to make a successful children's periodical. "A magazine for children can have no policy" Dodge once said. "Influence springs from something deeper than opinion."[15] And in a sense Dodge herself, especially in *St. Nicholas*'s formative years, was the source of the magazine's corporate personality. Her tastes, values, humor, zest, and common sense are plainly reflected in its pages. Though Dodge was a good businesswoman who frankly enjoyed the power she wielded, she preferred to be seen as a gracious, motherly caretaker rather than as a purveyor of a commercial product. This appealing image, serving both her audience's needs and her editorial purposes, was a key factor in the extraordinary and immediate success of the new magazine with its various publics.

Any periodical is by nature a mixed genre, with a diversity of voices. It is open-ended, discontinuous in form, full of gaps and dissonances. The editor's role is to provide some measure of closure, order, and continuity to the reader's experience of a periodical over time. One way in which a certain consistency can be enforced over the years is through the selectivity over content exercised by an editor possessing definite personal tastes. Dodge, as we shall see in chapter 8, had a good deal of influence on contributors and followed a policy of rewriting and cutting pieces to house standards. Her name and editorial presence provided a unifying element to the different issues in a given year, and the seasonal pattern of attention to various holidays and activities gave a familiar rhythm and shape to each successive volume.

Dodge's commitment to pleasing her readers and keeping them interested led her to reproduce elements that proved popular and to develop devices to link one issue to the next. She gradually acquired a stable of house authors whose names could guarantee sales and encouraged them to write serials and articles in series.

Moreover, she developed departments and participation schemes that involved readers in the shaping of the magazine itself. Perhaps most important, Dodge addressed a clearly defined model audience with which readers were invited to identify and thereby established for them the very vantage point from which they were to read the magazine.

"Jack in the Pulpit" and the "Letter-Box"

In the letter to Roswell Smith that became her article on the ideal children's magazine, Dodge had suggested that a warm, "jolly, sympathetic hand-to-hand personage who is sure to turn up here and there in every number" might well be a crucial factor in such a magazine's success. (Dodge had created such a figure at *Hearth and Home* in "Uncle Tim," whose mail, she boasted to Horace Scudder in 1869, had included about 400 letters from children.)[16] Dodge's "Jack in the Pulpit" feature gave *St. Nicholas* a smiling human face and allowed her to speak directly to readers without seeming priggish or preachy. Beginning in the first issue, Dodge presented her readers with a two-page spread headed by an engraving featuring a wildflower—a huge jack-in-the-pulpit—surrounded by children. From within the "pulpit" formed by the flower emerges a smiling, bespectacled personage to whom the children listen. "Jack," though a male figure, looks suspiciously like an affectionate caricature of Dodge. Popular as Dodge's curious editorial persona was from the very first issue, it seems that the ambiguous nature of Jack puzzled some readers, and Dodge responded to the question of who—or what—Jack was supposed to be in typical teasing fashion in her column for November 1875: "That reminds me: Am I a real Jack-in-the-Pulpit? you have asked—a true plant, growing and preaching out in the sunshine? Well, perhaps no. Perhaps yes. This much is certain: I *do* live in the sunshine; I *do* try to grow; and I *do* love to talk to the boys and girls of *ST. NICHOLAS*—to open their eyes and their minds by pointing out all sorts of queer truths here, there, and yonder—and to put into their hearts grateful loving thoughts toward the Giver of all Good. So, my darlings, if you're satisfied with this explanation, I am."[17]

"Jack-in-the Pulpit" maintains a faint fiction that its interlocutor dwells in a pretty meadow near a schoolhouse, the occupants of which frequently wander through the field, where they can meet and listen to Jack. The voice Dodge gives Jack is a warm, rather maternal one that addresses readers as "darlings," "chicks," or "dears." Though such terms can easily seem arch or coy to a modern ear, Jack's brisk manner, humor, and energy usually cut the sweetness enough to make it palatable. Jack is a conduit of information and advice, rather than a figure of daunting authority. Typically, he relays to the boys and girls of his audience what he has heard on the wind or picked up in the meadow. This stance helped Dodge to give her young readers a certain amount of "psychological space," probably more than many writers of the time would have granted. She wanted them to feel comfortable with the magazine, and she sought to pass on her own values without stifling or overwhelming her readers.

To lend variety and flexibility to the feature, Dodge added a couple of alternative personae, "Deacon Green" and the "Little Schoolma'am." The Deacon she characterized as a figure of some authority: "Deacon Green always hits the nail on the head, I'm told," and "He's a right, smart, good man, I'm sure, and knows what he's talking about."[18] But both the Deacon and the Little Schoolma'am occasionally make mistakes or are the subject of gentle teasing. The Schoolma'am is a figure Dodge brought along from *Hearth and Home*; she proves convenient for introducing information that might not readily have come Jack's way. (For example, she tells the boys and girls about "her" visit to Lewis Carroll, detailing what Dodge had experienced on her own recent trip to England.)

The department was Dodge's "own especial joy and pride," and the personae she created for it took on a life of their own. After Dodge's death, Fayal Clarke said:

> It is no betrayal of a confidence, now, to reveal that Mrs. Dodge was herself "Jack-in-the-Pulpit," "Deacon Green," and the "Little Schoolma'am" all in one. These were very actual and charming personages, however, to the boys

and girls of that time. Like Shakespeare's characters to children of a larger growth, they were quite as "real" as many of the living, breathing folk whose voices we hear and whose hands we touch. There was never so delightful a department for young readers as "Jack-in-the-Pulpit," nor one so endeared by matchless wit and wisdom to every youthful heart. (Clarke 1905, 1065)

The format of "Jack-in-the-Pulpit" was that of a miscellany. After a sprightly greeting and often some comment on the weather or time of year, Jack would present a series of tidbits: curious facts of natural history, jokes, poems, questions to research, quotations, letters, editorial comments, and nuggets of moral advice. Despite the frequent and gentle "sermonettes," the subject matter of the department ranged well beyond traditional "conduct of life" concerns. Jack never threatened his readers and often made common cause with them against the strictures of their elders. In one issue Jack complained in mock exasperation about the magazine's publishers, who insisted on putting out an August issue despite the incredible heat, and told the children to go out and play instead of reading it. (Dodge then presented a delicious parody of her usual Jack column, an elaborate in-house joke aimed at the parents she knew read her magazine almost as carefully as their children did.)[19]

A list of topics will show the range of interests the department managed to serve: current events, history, mythology, nature studies, popular anthropology, religion. But no mere list can convey the infectious curiosity, freshness, and excitement Dodge brought to each subject. When Jack asked a question about whether dogs and other animals favor one paw or the other, readers were invited to observe their pets in action and to report on what they found out. Often Jack would raise a question and ask the children to do library research and let him know what they found out. Readers soon discovered, to their intense delight, that their answers were printed in the magazine, and that they had become not only readers of a magazine but members of a club, a community of readers called into being by Dodge.

Although the "Jack" column from the outset published occasional letters from readers, in March 1874 Dodge began the "Letter-Box," another department that fostered this activity even more vigorously. In 1867 Dodge had advised Horace Scudder that "your only certain way of receiving *bona fide* letters from girls and boys is to introduce a correspondence or Letter-Box department—but is it a desirable thing for the children?"[20] The key to Dodge's doubt on the subject was probably her strong concern that children ought not to be encouraged to become self-conscious. She was always wary of prodigies and considered it her duty to avoid doing anything that might spoil the natural unaffectedness that for her was one of the charms of childhood. But Dodge soon learned that correspondence from her readers could be used to serve many purposes, and she found that she could do a good deal to offset the effects of celebrity on her young correspondents through the way she selected, edited, and responded to their letters.

The letters printed in *St. Nicholas*, whether in "Jack" or the "Letter-Box," were carefully chosen and modified to serve the editor's purposes. Children's errors were not preserved because they sounded cute; nor were the children subjected to lectures on their spelling or grammar. Letters selected for publication seem to have been chosen not because they represented some fine strain of youthful sensibility but because they said something in a natural and interesting way. A contemporary reviewer observed the "Letter-Box" to be a model for such departments in juvenile magazines: "The letters printed are worth it, and those condensed are not only judiciously but kindly so; the editor's treatment of the children is gentle, encouraging, and pleasantly regardful of the 'pet' beauties of their literary efforts, in a way that has not been equaled since Peter Parley's time,—nor then, for that matter."[21]

These letters created for Dodge's entire readership a model response that validated certain attitudes and interests, providing a pattern of reaction readers would come to find normative. They were encouraged to feel part of a closely bonded group whose members shared not only a favorite magazine but an earnest determination to educate themselves and one another, to engage actively with life, to make and do things. In the many letters that

say the same things—"I love *St. N.*," "I have subscribed for X
years," "I live in X"—and then add some particulars that set the
respondent apart from others, readers express both pleasure in
the sense that they share feelings and tastes with many of their
peers and confidence that their individual differences will be no
barrier to acceptance in the *St. Nicholas* family. And Dodge made
it clear to her readers that it was not the purchase of a subscription that made one a member of this group: letters were welcome
from any readers, whether they subscribed to the journal, read it
in libraries, or heard it read to them in school.

Sometimes Dodge used "Jack-in-the-Pulpit" or the "Letter-Box"
to promote the sort of reading of the magazine she wanted. She
would direct readers' attention to something that might otherwise
be too easily passed over, such as Lucy Larcom's essay on the
"Midsummer Poets," or she might provide gossip about an author,
such as her revelation in one issue that one of their readers'
favorite writers of adventure fiction, John Townsend Trowbridge,
had been a real hero, saving a life at the risk of his own. And
occasionally she used this space to draw readers' attention to
some good cause that needed their help—for instance, the Hans
Christian Andersen Fund or a hospital for children that needed
money or books. The "Letter-Box" and "Jack-in-the-Pulpit" also
provided Dodge with an opportunity to look back and comment,
explain, or apologize for something in a previous issue; she could
explain, for example, that Jack in a past issue might have made
a mistake about the whereabouts of Benjamin Franklin's birth.
And these departments allowed her to stir up interest in something slated to appear in the future—as when she noted in December 1875 that Deacon Green thought there should be a "Young
Contributors' Department" in the next issue.

Concerned with pleasing her young readers, Dodge polled them,
in September 1881, about the direction they wanted the journal
to take. She thanked them for the enormous outpouring of letters
that followed, telling her "in frank, hearty boy-and-girl fashion,
just the stories and pictures they liked best, and of what special
things they wished to have more." Dodge's comments on the results of her "Letter-Box" poll show her awareness of the mixed

nature of her audience. "ST. NICHOLAS," she observed, "is the servant and friend of young folk of all classes and ages from seven to seventeen," and she expressed her concern that everyone who subscribed should find "a considerable part of every number exactly suited to his or her tastes." But while she wanted to satisfy her readers' immediate desires, she also wanted to stretch their imaginations and provide material for them to grow on. She advised them, "You will find that, in this hurrying, busy, nineteenth-century life of ours, your present tastes will change or new tastes develop more rapidly than you can now imagine, and ST. NICHO-LAS, if it is truly to be your magazine, must keep pace with, and even anticipate your growth."[22]

Dodge wanted her readers to know how seriously she took their advice, but she also made it plain that *St. Nicholas*'s standards would not be compromised. And from time to time she spoke frankly to her audience about the abundance of sensational trash being offered to young readers of the time. Dodge was appalled by what she saw as the damage bad reading could do to children, and in one "Jack-in-the-Pulpit" column she told the story of a boy who hid a book whenever his father came along, and advised the boy never to read what he had to be ashamed of:

> Bad reading is a dangerous poison; and I, for one, would like to see the poisoners—that is, the men who furnish it—punished like any other murderers;—yes, and more,—for it's worse to kill the soul than to kill the body.
>
> In my opinion, parents are not half watchful enough in this matter, and if I were you young folks, I wouldn't stand it.[23]

But however Dodge might fulminate against the adults who provided sensational reading matter to young readers, she was gentleness itself to one reader, a little girl who found herself fascinated by the popular novel *St. Elmo* by Augusta Jane Evans. The child confessed that it "was not a good book for me; but I could not stop. It seemed as though it had some strange power, which, when I commenced it, kept me from stopping, and held fast to me until I had finished it." Dodge did not scold or criticize; instead, she suggested a lively and challenging reading list— Alcott, MacDonald, Stowe, Dickens, Thackeray, and Scott—and encouraged her precocious young reader to get in touch with the "Ladies Society for the Encouragement of Study at Home" for further guidance.[24]

During the 1880s, Dodge's conduct of the "Jack-in-the-Pulpit" column gradually began to change. Perhaps, having established the tone, manner, and relationship with her audience so thoroughly, and with the addition of other departments and special avenues for reader interaction, Dodge no longer needed the "Jack" feature so much. Perhaps the press of other activities prevented her from giving the column full attention. But at this time the department began more and more to feature the work of outside contributors who were paid rather nominal sums. In 1891 artist and poet Oliver Herford wrote to Fayal Clarke from France, desperately claiming he didn't dare leave his lodgings until he could pay his landlord. He tried to sell Clarke a short piece for the magazine, and when Clarke apparently offered him $8.00 to put it in "Jack-in-the-Pulpit," Herford asked the kindhearted editor to consider a revised version and, if it still did not suit, to send it along for him to another magazine.[25] During the later years of Dodge's editorship, the "Jack" feature appeared less often and relied more on such contributed material; then, with the January 1896 issue, it ceased appearing altogether.

Planning Issues

Dodge was very much aware that each issue of a magazine had to be carefully shaped, and that variety, balance, devices to engage readers' participation and to catch their interest in future issues were all-important. She had to think in terms not only of a single issue but of a volume, and a run of volumes that would each lead naturally from one to the next. Shaping *St. Nicholas* for more than three decades demanded imagination, arduous work, careful attention to what the audience wanted, and the courage to take significant risks. But Dodge was born for this work, as her friend

Lu Runkle once said. She loved the challenges of the editorial game and played it with enthusiasm and great skill.

Dodge's correspondence reveals how difficult it was for an editor to make individual issues of a miscellany come out just as they were planned. Her mentor Horace Scudder frequently complained about the way an issue would get away from him. In 1867 Scudder wrote Dodge about a forthcoming issue of the *Riverside* that he found "heavy and lumbering" and in need of "sprightliness and more downright fun." He confided that he found it very hard to "steer the magazine: It sometimes gets the bit between the teeth and rushes firmly into some marsh or other."[26]

Like Scudder, Dodge made a serious attempt to balance the contents of each issue between "instructive matter" and more entertaining material, and between serials and complete stories. And she was especially aware of the importance of ending a single year's volume in the most interesting way possible so as to ensure the renewal of subscriptions or the purchase of the next volume. In July 1877, while working on the October issue that would end the subscription year, she wrote to her publisher complaining that she couldn't find room for another nonfiction piece in the issue: "Already on account of being obliged to put in certain articles, serials etc. the number is overburdened with instructive matter & too scantily supplied with complete stories—and it is very important as you know for us to end the volume as *interestingly* to the children as possible. Mr. [Donald Grant] Mitchell's paper is delightful, but it is not a story."[27]

Dodge relied on serialization to build audience loyalty, and from *St. Nicholas*'s earliest days its advertising focused on serial offerings, especially fiction, ranging from 12-part novels to shorter pieces complete in 2 or 3 installments. For much of her long, serialized fiction, Dodge looked for well-established authors whose names would help sell the magazine. Louisa May Alcott had already made a great popular success with *Little Women* before she wrote *Eight Cousins, Under the Lilacs,* and *Jack and Jill* for Dodge. John Townsend Trowbridge, who had become available as an author when his own periodical, *Our Young Folks*, was absorbed by *St. Nicholas*, was invited to New York by Roswell

Smith and asked to continue the adventures of his popular hero
Jack Hazard for the *St. Nicholas* audience. Trowbridge, though
at first unhappy over losing his editorial post at *Our Young Folks*,
soon found his new freedom to write and sell where he wished
very pleasant. Although the initial strategy of keeping Trowbridge's name prominent in the pages of *St. Nicholas* reflected the
editors' desire to keep the audience of *Our Young Folks* happy
during the period of transition, Trowbridge became a regular contributor to *St. Nicholas*, which published a number of his novels
and his "Bass Cove Sketches."

Dodge was skillful at cutting long works for serialization and
was trusted by many authors to make crucial divisions. It was not
uncommon for authors to say to her, as Sarah Orne Jewett did of
a story, "I have separated it into three parts, but it will make four
just as well."[28] In the early days Dodge was careful to complete
an entire novel within a single year's volume, a necessary step
because bound copies of each volume were sold separately. After
volume 7, when the annual volumes were divided into two parts,
Dodge tried to arrange matters so that the serials could, when
possible, appear in one six-issue bound part. But later she experimented with running serials across volumes so as to entice readers to subscribe for another year. The cleverness with which
Dodge handled serialization was only emphasized by the failure
of Fayal Clarke's later experiment of publishing one long, self-
contained piece of fiction in each issue. Although Clarke arranged
for a tie-in publication by the Century Company of some of the
pieces, both the balance and the variety of the individual issues
suffered so much that the experiment was short-lived.

Of course, even a casual reading of *St. Nicholas* during Dodge's
tenure reveals that as an editor she had blind spots and failures
of taste and judgment, the most serious of which is evident in the
magazine's treatment of class, race, and the culture of ethnic
minorities. Irish, Italian, Chinese, and other immigrants, blacks
and Native Americans were often depicted in text and illustration
in demeaning stereotypes. And when a member of one of these
groups was presented sympathetically in a story or poem, the
piece was often marred by a patronizing, condescending tone.

In January of 1881 Dodge printed a story called "Nedawi" written by " 'Bright Eyes,' named by her white friends *Susette La Flesche* . . . a noble-hearted young lady, devoted to the cause of her people, and eager in the hope that our government will yet deal fairly with the Indian as with the white man." Dodge reprinted in the "Letter-Box" excerpts from a "friendly" letter Bright Eyes had written to her. The letter gives a sense of what it might have felt like for a young reader outside the white middle-class to read *St. Nicholas*. There is clearly much pain in it, and a strong desire to see her own people and their way of life honestly and respectfully depicted.

> I have never attempted writing a story, and fear it is an impossible thing for me, but I can, at least, try. . . . It seems so hard to make white people believe that we Indians are human beings of like passions and affections with themselves: that it is as hard for us to be good as it is for them,—harder, for we are ignorant,—and we feel as badly when we fail as they do. That is the reason I have written my story in the way I have. . . . If I were only at home I could write many things that would be interesting to white people, as grandmother remembers when they saw the first white men, and when there were no houses at all. None of our family speak English, excepting my sisters and myself, and it is delightful to hear father, mother, and grandmother tell their thrilling adventures, and speak of the many changes that have come since grandmother was a young girl. . . .
>
> It would be so much better for my people if the white people had a more thorough knowledge of them, because we have felt deeply the results of their ignorance of us. ("Letter-Box," *SN* 9.3 [January 1881]: 252)

Departments

To provide diversity within each issue and yet also give readers a sense of continuity, Dodge invented familiar, recurring features, departments, organizations, and participatory activities. She tried to provide something for everyone, balancing fact and fantasy, the interests of older and younger children, boys and girls. Each department served a special interest, and a sharp eye was kept on reader response, which often dictated how long a department would continue.

The department "For Very Little Folk" (1873–99) offered simple, often-didactic, but amusing stories for the youngest readers. It was lavishly illustrated and at first (though not subsequently) printed in large type. Dodge wrote many of the pieces for this department under her own name or as "Joel Stacy," a favorite pseudonym. Dodge's collection *Baby Days* (1877) is largely a selection of the best pieces from this department. Other departments focused on special interests, such as "Nature and Science for Young Folks" (1890–1930), "Current Events" (1898–99), and "Work and Play for Young Folk" (1883–86).

In the 1870s and 1880s two highly popular organizations for readers were formed. One was the Bird Defenders, inspired by C. C. Haskins's article offering a program for protecting wild birds. Haskins asked readers to enlist in the cause, and Dodge, in issue after issue, printed the names of those who joined the effort. Her own interest in natural history and her commitment to encouraging children's active participation in science projects made natural history features especially prominent throughout her editorship. In 1880 she printed a piece in which Harlan H. Ballard asked readers to join the Agassiz Association to promote the collection of natural objects. The association quickly enlisted a huge membership, with many active local chapters. A distinguished array of scientists, impressed by the quality of the association's work, helped to answer reader queries and judge contests. The Agassiz Association was so successful that its extensive reports finally outgrew the magazine and a separate publication had to be created for its members, though Dodge continued to take pride in promoting its activities and publishing its annual reports.

Probably the best-known department of *St. Nicholas* was the section of the magazine set aside for the reports of the St. Nicholas League, a group founded in November 1899 to help readers study the best that had been thought and written, learn more about nature, participate in an active outdoor life, and engage in patriotic activities and campaigns to protect the oppressed, whether human or animal. Membership in the league was free. The league encouraged local chapters to form discussion groups and offered a number of popular competitions in writing, photography, drawing, and puzzle-solving, with gold and silver badges for the winners, cash prizes, and an honor roll. Dodge hired Albert Bigelow Paine to plan and monitor these activities and to handle the vast correspondence they entailed.

Paine took his responsibilities seriously, and under his care the league's membership soon grew to 40,000. His papers, preserved at the Huntington Library, reveal that he gave generously of his time, offering readers criticism of their writing and serving as a literary mentor, sometimes for many years. One reader wrote to Paine, "It is a fine thing for a boy to be advised in the work that he loves by someone (*the one*) to whom he looks for criticism."[29] A winner of a gold badge from the league wrote; "I thank St. Nicholas heartily. I have learned to write concisely, and I have learned from you that the prize is not all."[30] This same boy, when he turned 17, submitted a story for the main section of the magazine. Paine criticized it, but the young author decided to appeal to Dodge personally in terms that show how well he had internalized her own standards of selection. His letter urges her to "remember, as you read it, the story is *not written* for grown-ups—with all their witty criticisms—I wrote it for the little people and because I love to write," and he goes on to tell her that his little sisters understood and approved it.[31] Dodge evidently could not resist his letter, and published the story. Many other budding authors found their first encouragement in the league, and one mark of the influence Dodge has had on American literature is the impressive list of well-known writers and artists whose names first appeared in print in the honor rolls.[32]

Aside from her editorial presence in "Jack-in-the-Pulpit" and "The Letter-Box," Dodge occasionally spoke directly to her readers in the opening pages of the magazine, as she did in the first issue. And she often addressed readers directly in book reviews and short pieces on reading and literature. Occasionally she commissioned essays on reading from people she trusted to advise her young readers soundly. She persuaded her former editor at *Hearth and Home*, Donald G. Mitchell, to talk to boys and girls about great writers in a series published during the magazine's first five years. Among the figures discussed were Swift, Bunyan, Dickens, and Defoe.

One department, "The Treasure Box of Literature," reprinted famous poems, sketches, and short stories that might not ordinarily be presented to young readers. Dodge reserved the right to omit an occasional verse or paragraph when doing so seemed in her audience's interest, but she believed her readers needed something to grow on and wanted to make them better acquainted with the classics, which she felt could be made accessible if presented in the right way.

Dodge not only read her young readers' letters carefully but liked to talk to children, and listened to what they said. A story in one of Dodge's letters to her editorial mentor, Horace Scudder, illustrates her curiosity about what goes on in children's minds when they read. Dodge, at a vacation hotel, decided to see how one of the young guests responded to the latest issue of Scudder's *Riverside Magazine*. The little boy was bright, but she was unable to "conduct him further" into the magazine than the frontispiece, a rather inept engraving of a puppy in front of a fireplace, at which the boy gazed "in perfect absorption," insisting that Dodge not turn the page. When she asked why he wanted to be shown this picture so often, he asked with surprise whether she didn't like it, too. Puzzled by this reaction, Dodge probed further, until she discovered that the boy interpreted the picture as a dangerous scene in which the fire tongs were about to fall on the helpless dog. "This then," she wrote to Scudder, "was the point of attraction. Did you suspect that this charming idyl of a frontispiece had any such tragic element in it?" It was like Dodge to want very much to know "the point of attraction" in the picture for the child, to take the trouble to uncover the misreading—and also like her to tell Scudder, teasingly, how his best editorial intentions had missed their mark for at least one reader.[33]

Dodge knew that what children would choose if left to their own devices would be different from what she or Scudder would choose for them. "But," she said, "do we not undervalue 'the wisdom of babes' when we set up too steadfastly our own standards in such matters? Perhaps the children are right, in some things, and we are wrong. A suspicion of this would forbid my thrusting a story of Good Bobby at a little fellow who was clamorous for Grimm."[34] Though Dodge's own sons had devoured Oliver Optic and Mayne Reid, she knew that the same hunger for excitement, danger, and heroism also drew her boys to Shakespeare and Tennyson when those authors' work were presented in the right way.

In 1874 Dodge was asked to write a book directing children to good reading. At the time she was too pressed by editorial duties to accept the proposal. The interest of the project lay for her in the fact that the "acknowledged classics for children are not relatively as fixed or as super-excellent as the classics for grown people." She thought it important that children be directed to good reading. It was a task that "ought" to be done if the right person could be found. It is unfortunate that Scribner's didn't pursue the matter further, for everything we know of Dodge's conduct of *St. Nicholas* suggests that she was surely the very "reverent, sunny child-loving mentor who could meet the case."[35]

8

"But is it right for *St. Nick?*"

The Prospectus

In the spring of 1873 Dodge sent an announcement to prospective authors outlining the requirements of the new and as-yet-unnamed magazine for children she would edit. Significantly, the first thing contributors were told was that the new periodical was to be "profusely illustrated by the best artists at home and abroad." The "look" of *St. Nicholas* when it appeared—paper, graphics, layout—would be fresh and new. Dodge worked closely with authors and artists through every stage of their work, from the inception of a project to its appearance in print. She could rely on the generosity of publishers committed to the highest standards in design and printing. And she was fortunate to have available the expertise of Alexander Drake, who had excellent contacts in the art world and whose services as art director she shared with *Scribner's Monthly* and later the *Century*. In the course of time Dodge and Drake would bring to the pages of *St. Nicholas* the bold drawings of Howard Pyle, the quaint silhouettes of John Bennett, the elegant sketches of Reginald Birch, and the lively and original work of Palmer Cox and Gellett Burgess.[1]

Dodge had outlined her ideas about the role of art in a children's magazine in her letter to Roswell Smith printed in *Scribner's Monthly*: the pictures should have variety, "they should be heartily conceived and well executed; and they must be suggestive, attractive and epigrammatic" ("CM," 352–54). Dodge wanted illustrations to "cause a whole tangle of interrogation-marks in the child's mind." She felt that the best pictures for children would speak for themselves. A picture, she said, "if it be only the picture of a cat," "must be so like a cat that it will do its own purring, and not sit, a dead, stuffed thing, requiring the editor to purr for it." Dodge loathed what she called "editorial dribbling over inane pictures" and thought "the time to shake up a dull picture is when it is in the hands of the artist and engraver, and not when it lies, a fact accomplished, before the keen eyes of the little folk" ("CM," 353).

The prospectus for Scribner and Company's new journal warned contributors that pious sermonizing was to be avoided. The magazine was to be "entirely unsectarian in character," and would "avoid anything like formal teaching or preaching." Pleasure would be its keynote: "The spirit of mirthfulness shall be invoked from the first, and all good things fresh, true, and child-like, heartily commended, while every way to juvenile priggishness shall be bolted and barred as far as the management can effect." The terms *fresh, true,* and *childlike* were perhaps deliberately vague. What Dodge meant would be clarified in practice by the image of themselves her readers would find reflected in the fiction she chose for them and in the letters and contributions she selected for publication in the "Letter-Box" or "Jack-in-the-Pulpit" features (*P*).

The new journal was to instruct its readers "indirectly." There was to be no "wearisome spinning out of facts, no rattling of the dry bones of history" ("CM," 353). Some years later, when Horace Scudder proposed to add a life of Washington in serial form to a year's schedule that already included a massive history of the Civil War, Dodge would object on behalf of her readers: "The poor little things study hard at school & rightly expect to be entertained by their magazine—and we all the while are smuggling in so much valuable information! Sometimes I feel as if every useful & instructive paper in 'St. Nicholas' will be brought up against me on the Day of Judgment, even if some wise angel in spectacles *does* pat me approvingly for my 'good work.' But don't tell anyone this."[2] If and when facts made their entrance in *St. Nicholas* they were not to be sugarcoated or couched in baby talk but instead to be made "entertaining and interesting."[3] Dodge insisted on accuracy, however, so far as it was in "her power," for she thought "a bad moral effect on young readers" resulted from encountering a "careless, unconscientious" attitude toward reporting the facts in print.[4]

The lavish manner in which Scribner and Company was going to support the new project was signaled in the prospectus both by the promise of a liberal pay scale and by the description of Dodge herself as spending "a portion of the summer in Europe, gleaning materials and securing contributions for the new venture." Meanwhile, American writers were solicited to contribute "the very best reading matter for boys and girls": "brief, bright, entertaining original stories, sketches and other articles for young folks from five to sixteen years." What Scribner and Company meant in practice by the terms *bright, entertaining,* and *"original"* was made clear by the standard set by Dodge and Frank Stockton, who between them furnished two-thirds of the material for the first issue (*P*).

Selecting Contributors

Dodge's ambition was to bring the best writers in the English-speaking world to her young readers, and her letters and papers reveal how diligently she worked to do this. Dodge was adept at recognizing new talent and artful in persuading literary lions to write for her new journal. The "liberal" pay scale for authors and artists announced in the *St. Nicholas* prospectus was a potent attraction, but so were Dodge's sympathetic appreciation of her contributors' work and her readiness with just the right encouraging word (*P*).

When artist-writer John Bennett was young, ill, and living a precarious hand-to-mouth existence, he sent her a whimsical short story, got a cordial response to it, and within a year was asked to become a regular contributor. "Rates of pay," said Bennett, "exceeded that from any other source." But what meant more to him was the fact that "not a manuscript . . . went to or was returned from St. NICHOLAS offices without some word from Mrs. Dodge. With every acceptance, and with every infrequent declination, she invariably sent some message of encouraging criticism, helpful suggestion, or stimulating praise." Forty-five years later Bennett said he had "never met the same cordial recognition elsewhere."[5]

John Greenleaf Whittier was a distinguished elder poet who needed no showcase in *St. Nicholas*, but Dodge was determined to persuade him to write for the boys and girls. Her secret weapon in this campaign was Whittier's close friend Celia Thaxter, whose letters to Dodge detail their ceaseless campaign to lure Whittier into the *St. Nicholas* fold. Although he resisted for a time, he was ultimately brought to say that if he would write for anyone it would be Dodge. He continued to contribute to the journal until his death and came to count Dodge "as a dear personal friend."[6]

Dodge often sent likely contributors bound volumes of *St. Nicholas*, a gracious present that also served to give them a sense of her requirements in terms of tone, manner, pacing (especially when serialization might be a consideration), layout, and the options in illustration. While on a visit to Boston, Dodge called on Henry Wadsworth Longfellow, leaving with him a couple of bound copies of *St. Nicholas* and following up with a charming letter, to which Longfellow replied: "It is impossible to resist the 'affectuoso grido'—the affectionate appeal of your letter. So powerful is it, that I send you two pieces instead of one."[7]

Dodge herself had a wide acquaintance among New York's writers, journalists, artists, and intellectuals but was always willing to employ the help of her colleagues at Scribner's and the Century Company. Though they were not, strictly speaking, employed by *St. Nicholas*, Dodge was also to find many of those who worked for Scribner and Company fast friends and useful allies—people like Clarence Buel, Will Carey, L. Frank Tooker, Robert Underwood Johnson, and, of course, the *Century*'s editor, "Watsey" Gilder, an old friend of Dodge's from her Mapleridge days. Tensions between Dodge and Gilder arose now that each was in charge of a magazine hungry for copy, but they maintained a cooperative working relationship and shared with remarkable generosity and consideration a strikingly similar list of contributors. Though one of Dodge's greatest contributions to children's literature of the period was her ability to persuade prominent authors for adults to write for children—and to teach them, when necessary, how to do so—access to the contributors to one of New York's most prestigious and well-paying periodicals for adults was a secret of her success.

Roswell Smith, founder of *St. Nicholas* and director of the Century Company that published it, represented Dodge in discussions with William Dean Howells (Wright 1979, 132); and Richard Watson Gilder, of the *Century*, served as an eager intermediary between Dodge and George MacDonald (Wright 1979, 130–31). When Kipling—whom Dodge wanted to enlist for *St. Nicholas*—arrived in New York, his first engagement was a luncheon at a private club from which women were excluded. But Dodge knew how to array her forces. She sent Will Carey, an engaging colleague from the *Century*, to sound Kipling out. Carey made the approach and went straight home to pen a note to Dodge indicating that Kipling *was* interested in writing for her. Meanwhile, Dodge's friend and former assistant editor, Frank Stockton, had already dropped in at her home to report his version of what had happened at the luncheon (Wright 1979, 174).

When a potential contributor—even a good friend like George MacDonald—proved to Dodge that he simply could not write for the boys and girls of *St. Nick*, Dodge was firm about not asking for more work out of politeness or obligation. MacDonald was the idol of her colleague Richard Watson Gilder, who took every opportunity to press MacDonald's work on her. But Dodge, for reasons she never made perfectly clear, felt his stories were not suited to American children. She said that she enjoyed them, and knew that most adults of her acquaintance did, but "the chance of getting one utterly away from" the needs of American children was so great that she hadn't the "courage to try the experiment" again. MacDonald had written one of her series of "Talks with

Boys," and "though stamped as his own & full of beauty" it "did not hit the mark at all." She said that she had "never found a young reader who cared for it in the least or even understood it." The problem, Dodge suggested, was that MacDonald had failed to find an appropriate voice in which to speak to American children. She objected not so much to what he said as to how he said it; "Literature is a grand masquerade, after all, and the masks are not 'ordered off' till the children are grown up." [8]

Cultivating Contributors

Louisa May Alcott

Dodge's correspondence reveals that her contributors not only asked for her professional advice but confided the details of numerous personal problems and concerns. She had a gift for friendship, a good deal of sensitivity to the individual needs of the writers and artists who worked for her, and a generous desire to help them. She worried about them, tried to promote their careers, saw to it that they were fairly and promptly paid, did them personal favors, entertained them, and socialized with them. A number of writers came to feel that Dodge herself was a marvelous audience. Perhaps this, together with her empathy for her young readers, explains her ability to get from each contributor "his or her best" (Clarke 1905, 1065).

Dodge's first approach to a contributor was often through a letter. She wanted very much to have a contribution from Louisa May Alcott in the first issues of *St. Nicholas*, but Alcott put her off, saying she was too busy with other work. Dodge's persistent letters finally won Alcott over, and "from 1874 on," Alcott "was to supply for *St. Nicholas* thirty-two narratives including three serials" (Stern, 338).

When she could, Dodge liked to meet with contributors, either in her office or at social gatherings. She and Alcott finally got together in 1875 when both "attended a Fraternity Club meeting, and the two successful women . . . shared confidences, Mrs. Dodge recalling how the Mapes girls—much like the March girls—had dramatized their childhood readings" (Stern, 339). As the two women came to know each other better, they found they had a good deal in common, and what began as a professional relationship became an affectionate friendship.

Though men she knew had offered their advice on the matter, it was Dodge to whom Alcott turned when she needed to find a good boardinghouse in New York where a woman could comfortably stay alone.[9] A strong bond of sympathy between the two women is reflected in their correspondence. They exchanged tender and eloquent letters of condolence when family members died and commiserated with each other during their frequent bouts of ill health. Although Dodge always needed copy and needed it on time, she was concerned about the painful and disabling hand condition that made the physical act of writing difficult for Alcott. She thus urged Alcott to take her time in recopying material[10] and in 1882, observing that "the manual labor of writing a long story is a serious thing, especially so if the MS. is to be copied after one's first fervor of composition has abated," suggested that Alcott might send rough drafts of the chapters of the serial she was working on to the *St. Nicholas* offices, so that fair copies could be made of them. Dodge promised not to look at the chapters until they were completed to the author's satisfaction but offered to pay for the serial in installments as the draft chapters arrived.[11]

Dodge also tried to help Alcott when her inspiration dried up. At one point she sent Alcott some appealing illustrations, in the hope that they might inspire a story idea or two. Alcott was delighted by the technique, which led to her *Spinning Wheel Stories*.[12] Their friendship withstood the bidding wars over Alcott's fiction by various publishers (including Dodge's colleagues at Scribner's), and Alcott felt free to pour out her distress at it all to Dodge in her letters.[13] Dodge, on her side, understood Alcott's special relationship with editor Thomas Niles of Boston's Roberts Brothers and was glad to arrange the appearance of Alcott's stories in *St. Nicholas* in such a way that they would enhance the sales of the subsequent collections published by Roberts.

Lucy Larcom

A sequence of early letters to Lucy Larcom shows Dodge first establishing that she had read Larcom's poetry with intelligent appreciation and then, letter by letter, building a personal relationship based on mutual trust and respect. In one early letter Dodge confessed to having a strong emotional reaction to one of Larcom's poems about motherhood and revealed that her own sons had filled the place of the husband, the lover, that her life had lacked. Dodge, who rarely spoke so unguardedly about her husband's death, even to close personal friends, concluded by saying that she hadn't intended to talk of her home life but was overcome by her reaction to Larcom's poem.[14]

Dodge's practical criticism to authors on their work in progress was often detailed and specific. Later letters to Larcom include requests for particular kinds of poetry Dodge wanted from her, careful critiques of work submitted, and hints on how best to meet the needs of the child audience. When Larcom sent her a poem Dodge didn't think up to standard, Dodge told her that the second verse lacked her "usual finish" and was "a little prosaic in expression and defective in metre." But Dodge was gentle and encouraging, and accepted the poem—providing Larcom would make the necessary changes.[15]

When Larcom wrote a series of articles introducing children to poetry, Dodge instructed her on what the pieces should contain and even the tone they should take—"light and gossipy, yet full of tender spirit and feeling."[16] The first article proved a bit of a disappointment, and Dodge firmly advised structural changes in the next one that would allow Larcom to catch the young readers' attention and lead "them into the subject with a clearer comprehension of its significance." And, she added tactfully, "You can do it so sweetly that it will not be stiff. Young folk are apt to skip poetry unless they are wooed in some such way."[17]

Rudyard Kipling

Catharine Morris Wright has told the story of how Dodge got Rudyard Kipling to address the *St. Nicholas* audience (Wright

1974, 259–89). Dodge's correspondence with Kipling demonstrates a number of her talents as an editor. For one thing, that correspondence (probably) began when Kipling, as a schoolboy of 13, submitted to *St. Nicholas* a poem called "The Dusky Crew" for publication. The poem was not very good, and Kipling later claimed to Dodge that some member of his family must have sent it to her. Dodge apparently scrawled "Poem really too poor to use. Refused as courteous as I could" on the envelope and tucked it away in her desk (Wright 1974, 262).

That courteous reply was a good investment for Dodge, because when Kipling came to New York many years later and was approached on Dodge's behalf, he said "that it was the height of his ambition to be invited to contribute to *St. Nicholas* by Mrs. Dodge."[18] Dodge wasted no time in issuing that invitation. But when, according to Fayal Clarke, she met Kipling for the first time and he asked, "Aren't you going to ask me to write for *St. Nicholas?*" she offered the "bantering reply," "I am not sure that you can! Do you think you are equal to it?" She was always careful to impress on writers who usually wrote for adults that writing for a child audience was a very different and sometimes more difficult matter. But Kipling answered her teasing question with an eager "Oh, but I must and I shall! for my sister and I used to scramble for ST. NICHOLAS every month, when I was a kid" (Clarke 1905, 1064). Having been a member of the *St. Nicholas* audience, he understood how demanding writing for it might be, and told Dodge that these readers were "a People a good deal more important and discriminating" than the adult audience he'd written things like "Wee Willie Winkie" for, "a peculiar People with the strongest views on what they like & dislike and I shall probably have to make three or four false starts before I can even get the key I hope to start on."[19]

Kipling sent Dodge a poem by a friend whom he would only identify as HJH, and Dodge, assuming that this was a pseudonym of Kipling's, offered him $250 for it, only to find out that HJH was not, after all, Kipling. Though the matter was delicate, Dodge handled it lightly and charmingly, and Kipling responded with equal grace, offering to take less for the poem, an offer promptly taken up by the practical, business-minded editor. Kipling also produced a story of his own, "The Potted Princess," and asked Dodge to read it "swiftly" to gauge if it were "quite right," for, he said, "it is a most important audience; and I can't afford to mess my pitch before them." He added that he would be happy to "revise or if necessary re-write or do another tale. Grown-ups are only grown-ups but a child is a child, you see."[20]

One of the most important things Dodge did for her regular contributors was to encourage them to explore the ideas they tentatively set out to her. Kipling, when he sent along his first story for her "most stern inspection," included a whole list of ideas for more stories to come, among them some of the essentials of what seven years later would become his novel *Kim*.[21] Her response to his first story and to the list of ideas for future work was ecstatic (perhaps a little more ecstatic than the story warranted, for here was an author who needed encouraging, and there would be time later to make a few suggestions, including a change in that irritating title), and Dodge, after taking care in generous fashion of the business details concerning payments and so forth, took the time to respond to his plans for future work:

No, I never did hear of the monkeys and the poison-stick, nor of that particular Noah's ark, nor of the . . . tam o'-shantered priest & the young English child.

But—. . . I yearn to. H.J.H. may not be a hog on dollars, but *St. Nicholas is* on stories from your pen. My cry is still for more, and the . . . prospect of an R.K. book of stories for young folk is most welcome both to Editors and publishers of *St. N.* I devoutly hope it will materialize in its own good time—. . . the sooner—the better. You shudderingly say our special public is particular to distraction, but you cannot conceive what a terror the . . . children become if an author who once pleases *them* . . . dares to stop! In short, why go back to the old folks at all? Any dry bones will do for them.[22]

Letter after letter from Kipling to Dodge poured out ideas for stories, and before long *St. Nicholas* and the Century Company had a whole set of *Jungle Book* stories that Dodge had teased and coaxed for. Dodge's hunch that better would be forthcoming than just the first story—whose title Kipling would not change—was sound. But interestingly enough, the last (and, Kipling thought, the funniest) of this group of stories, "The Servants of the Queen," was the only one Dodge felt she had to "turn down"—and turn it down she did, albeit in a "pretty letter."[23]

"But it is right for *St. Nick?*"

A phrase that crops up often in Dodge's correspondence with authors is: "But is it right for *St. Nick?*" As editor, Dodge undertook to interpret for her contributors the demands not only of the young readers of *St. Nicholas* but of a conservative audience of parents and teachers who wanted children to find in its pages role models of disciplined virtue and propriety. It was not easy to balance the claims of both audiences, but a close examination of Dodge's editorial correspondence and a comparative study of corrected manuscripts and their published versions will reveal something of what Dodge came to mean when she said something was "right" for her magazine.

Meeting the Needs of Young Readers

Dodge was sure she knew what children needed and wanted. She once said that she thought of all the young readers of a single magazine as having a "family likeness," and she prided herself on being able to help authors understand "for what set of little ones" they were writing.[24] She read her mail carefully and knew that *St. Nicholas*'s readers hated to be condescended to. When one author proposed to have an adult character say that in talking to children he would "put a little gilding on the pill," he received a firm memo telling him that "this expression, though perfectly appropriate in conversation with a grown person, would be rather resented by young readers."[25]

Dodge knew, too, that her young readers demanded writing that was well organized, direct, clear, and accurate. They enjoyed suspense but liked definite endings. Since the readership of the magazine varied in age, it was important that each piece of writing be carefully measured to the needs of the specific age-group for which it was designed. Although Dodge allowed writers a good deal of freedom on other matters, on this point she wrote, " 'independence must have its limits' since an article for the young loses or gains in value just in proportion as it is adapted to the age of the reader."[26]

Dodge was firm about the need for clear, uncluttered, reasonably short pieces in *St. Nicholas*, and though her contributors often protested about the difficulty of cutting their work to suit her specifications, she was not easily moved. In letter after letter Helen Hunt Jackson laments the impossibility of cutting one word more, but she does so anyway (Wright 1979, 111). The suave E. C. Stedman barely manages to veil his irritation at having to disguise the "amputations" Dodge has required but gallantly adds, "[I]f you think it still requires modifying—why *make any change* your Ladyship's experienced *wisdom may require.*"[27]

Meeting the Demands of the Adult Readership

As basic editorial policy, Dodge turned down for publication anything that in her view was overly didactic, sectarian, lachrymose, politically divisive, or morally dubious. Yet much of the most interesting material that came to her was problematic not for any of these reasons but simply because it included behavior, events, or language that some of her adult readers might view as setting a bad example for children. Aware of the restrictions under which Dodge worked, Robert Louis Stevenson hesitated to give her a story he had written, because his hero was a liar and he knew that might be a problem for her.[28] A letter to Dodge from Libbie Custer explains that she has added something to clarify the reason a child feels he is justified in taking someone else's chickens, but, knowing Dodge's situation, Custer is quick to add that the editor should feel free to take out the incident if she thinks readers' mothers would object.[29]

Frank Stockton reportedly complained about the supersensitivity of magazine publishers to criticism from the genteel public, saying that "one letter of protest from some damned nobody would raise more hell in a magazine's office than ten letters of praise from intelligent people."[30] And Samuel Chapin, one of Dodge's assistants, noted that in the *St. Nicholas* offices legend had it that a story once printed included an incident "in which children dare each other to stretch their mouths over a door-knob," a matter that "brought many frantic letters from irate mothers."[31]

The stress of constant complaints from readers made Dodge "very wary both in the subject matter of MSS., and in the matter of illustration." One standing joke in the office involved an artist's patient efforts to satisfy his editor's concerns for propriety:

> Mr. Sandham the artist made a picture for a story called, I think, "The Coward," in which on a picnic the rather sissi-fied [*sic*] young hero carries in his arms one of the girls of the party over a high railroad trestle on which they have been caught before an advancing train. Mr. Sandham's first effort was very dramatic and spirited as a picture but unfortunately the young girl's dress was being blown quite banner-like by the wind with a resultant display of too much ankle and lower limb. Mindful of caviling parents, Mrs. Dodge told Mr. Sandham that he must tone down the waving garments, with the result that after submitting three revisions of his drawing, the artist finally in despair submitted one in which the young girl's figure was depicted as an Egyptian mummy closely swathed in wrappings. No one enjoyed Mr. Sandham's humor more than Mrs. Dodge herself and the illustration finally reached a happy compromise.[32]

Dodge knew, of course, that her young readers might find a bit dull a magazine full of stories about moral paragons who lived in an ideal world. She once defended some characters of her own to Horace Scudder of the *Riverside*, saying, "Perhaps you may think that my children talk and act rather roughly—they certainly would shock *some* persons—but then I draw from life—and do we not owe some allegiance to naturalness and simple fact?" She understood, however, the editorial constraints under which Scudder sometimes had to work and, as a "meek and trustful" author, gave him permission to "prick the little folk up to a higher standard with the editorial pen" if he thought it necessary to do so.[33] As editor of *St. Nicholas*, Dodge often found herself forced to take similar measures, whether she liked it or not.

Dodge's tenure as editor of *St. Nicholas* coincided with the rise of realism in American literature. At this time "any of the realists—Boyesen, Clemens, Crane, Garland, Howells, James—would cheerfully have admitted that romance and romanticism were right for *St. Nicholas* because they were right for children."[34] But Dodge, in her own genteel way, was sympathetic to the realist impulse. (Even the fantasy in *St. Nicholas* had a down-to-earth quality to it.) She wanted to include not only fairy tales and fantasy in her magazine but local-color fiction, lively stories of ordinary life, and considerable biography and reportage.

Dodge's own attitude toward what the best in literary realism could bring her readers is suggested by "a lightly veiled act of literary warfare" she published in February 1887: "Little Effie's Realistic Novel," by Alice Marland Wellington Rollins (Saler and Cady, 167). In the story little Effie decides she should be able to write a realistic novel like Mr. Howells, but discovers it is harder to write realism than to write fantasy. She is told by her father:

> "I think you will find out, as you go on, that it requires a great deal more imagination to write a realistic novel than to write a fairy-tale; because the object of a realistic story is not to repeat common things but to interest people in common things; not to create uncommon things, but to show people that common things are not by any means so uninteresting as they seem at first sight. The realistic writer must see, not new things, but new qualities in things, and to do that he must have plenty of imagination." (Quoted in Saler and Cady, 168)

John Townsend Trowbridge's *His One Fault*

A memo in the Century Company files about John Townsend Trowbridge's serial story *His One Fault* will suggest the nature of the problem presented to the editors by lively, realistic children's fiction. In the memo Fayal Clarke reminds Trowbridge that Dodge has assured him of her "hearty appreciation & admiration of the story as a whole" and makes it clear that "the few modifications here suggested are asked for the *magazine version, on account of* the peculiar limitations & requirements of 'St. Nicholas.' " Certain incidents in the story must be modified when it is serialized: Trowbridge is asked to condense the story of an asthma attack and to "tone down" a cudgeling and a character's harsh treatment of his wife. The author is assured that "Mrs. Dodge appreciates the truth to nature and the dramatic value of these, as now described—if written for a book, or for older readers—but for 'St. Nicholas' the changes suggested must be an improvement."[35]

A comparison of the serialized version of *His One Fault* as printed in *St. Nicholas* and the novel as published in 1887 by Lee and Shepard of Boston and Charles T. Dillingham of New York will make clearer the implications of the modifications made by Trowbridge at the request of the editors at *St. Nicholas.* Trowbridge was a lively writer whose strength lay in creating action-filled plots rather than in any great subtlety of characterization. The protagonist of *His One Fault* is an appealing boy named Christopher (Kit) Downimede, whose basic intelligence and good-heartedness are overshadowed by "his one fault," heedlessness. The minor characters are stock figures given a touch of life by the arbitrary assignment of some colorful detail. The story is told in the third person, with Kit as a focal character during much of the action.

Kit never says a disrespectful word to an adult, but when his wayward fantasy about his uncle's asthma blends into the narrator's description of Uncle Gray's conversation "filled with the uninteresting music of what seemed a stirred-up swarm of bees in his chest" (Trowbridge, 119–20), and Aunt Gray is coolly described as "bald as a melon" until she has put on her "false hair" (Trowbridge, 25), the reader is invited to look at these well-meaning adults with—at best—a detached and faintly patronizing attitude. This sort of attitude clearly is not right for *St. Nicholas*, and the offending passages, targeted in Clarke's memo, have been carefully cut for the serialized version.

The cudgeling of young Kit by an older man, Eli Badger, was toned down by changing the description not of the beating itself but its aftermath. In the original version Trowbridge encourages the reader to assume that Eli has killed Kit, whose body is described as a "lifeless lump" (Trowbridge, 189) and a "limp form" (Trowbridge, 596). In the *St. Nicholas* version, in keeping with Dodge's tradition of treating necessary evils with dispatch and detachment, the violence remains, but the long-drawn-out suspense and some of the details (a bleeding nose, for example) are omitted.

Badger is shown to treat his wife with brutal indifference to her feelings. In the original version the cruel treatment of Mrs. Badger troubles Kit, "making him feel crushed and uncomfortable on her account" (Trowbridge, 204). In the *St. Nicholas* version Badger is still cruel to his wife, but Kit does not agonize over it, and less attention is drawn to the situation.

Another notation in Clarke's memo expresses concern about "mother's suggestion" (Clarke n.d.)—the young Widow Downimede's practical observation to her son about the uncle and aunt who have invited him to live with them: " 'They're getting old, and will soon have a good many dollars to leave to somebody,' the mother suggested. She was not mercenary, and yet she thought it best to speak plainly of the prospect before Christopher, in case he should accept Uncle Gray's proposal. 'It's a small farm, but a good one, and they have money at interest' " (Trowbridge, 13). In the *St. Nicholas* version this passage is omitted, rendering Mrs. Downimede a slightly more proper but less forthright and interesting character than she had been in Trowbridge's original conception.

Kit is a handsome 16-year-old who attracts the attention of two girls in the story. One, Elsie Benting, is intelligent, gentle, and friendly. She blushes in a ladylike way when Kit is around, takes his part when everyone is against him, and provides the conventional love interest for him. The other girl is the willful daughter of Eli Badger. Lydia Badger shares her father's "torrid" temperament and dotes on Kit in an embarassing fashion in the original version: "Whenever he looked up, as he could not help doing now and then, fascinated by her gaze, her large, blue eyes and full, red, open lips encouraged him with a sweet smile" (Trowbridge, 205). This sort of detail has been cut in the *St. Nicholas* version, the humor of the situation in which it places Kit perhaps being judged more appropriate for older readers.

There was apparently great pressure on Dodge to avoid presenting models of less-than-standard speech that young readers might imitate. In his memo Clarke told Trowbridge: "St Nicholas [*sic*] is seriously crippled in the use of dialect by the demands of parents & teachers for strictly grammatical language in the magazine." But recognizing the demands of literary realism, Clarke added that the only thing they could do was to "avoid extremes and try to be both natural & grammatical as far as possible." He thus asked for permission to "make such slight alterations in text as seem to us necessary to avoid too much criticism of the kind we have mentioned." The whole tone of the memo is regretful, but it firmly reiterates that Dodge and her staff knew what was right for *St. Nicholas*, and Clarke thoughtfully advised Trowbridge about a simple way of marking changes in his manuscript so that the original readings could easily be restored when the manuscript was submitted for publication in book form (Clark n.d.).

The editorial changes in the dialogue of *His One Fault* left enough of the dialect in Trowbridge's story to preserve the colorful quality of his characters' speech while rendering it much closer to standard English. Many of the changes dropped regional pronunciations reflected in spellings. And forbidden and ungenteel expressions like *ain't* were suppressed—even when used by rogues and villains. There seems to have been a special effort to cut colorful or original slang that might be imitated by young readers and reflect discredit on *St. Nicholas*. One expression apparently struck Clarke as a particularly dangerous example, for he made a special note in his memo about the villain's calling

Kit's mouth his "fly-trap" (Trowbridge, 72), a remark cut in the serialized version.

The many changes suggested by the editors at *St. Nicholas* made it possible for the magazine to publish the story without having to worry about parental objections. The alterations made the serialized version smoother, a little more elegant, and lent it a more genteel tone. Dodge once spoke admiringly of the way her publishers "Scribnerized" a book. And in a sense she and her colleagues gently "*St. Nicholas*ized" *His One Fault*. Kit remains a lovable boy, though heedless and forgetful, but his elders are a little less flawed and his own understanding of their limitations has been muted. His mother no longer has her eye on Uncle Gray's money, the farmer and his wife are more dignified figures, Eli Badger's violence is more lightly passed over, and less attention is given to Eli's treatment of his wife and daughter. The story remains colorful and lively,—a good example of the sort of story that made Trowbridge one of *St. Nicholas*'s most popular writers—but its rough edge has been blunted and it is not quite the same piece Trowbridge originally offered.

Dodge was certainly not alone in feeling pressure to avoid publishing dialectal material that might raise the objections of readers. Her colleague Richard Watson Gilder, editor of the *Century*, wrote to Hamlin Garland in 1890 explaining the restrictions under which he himself worked: "People who are trying to bring up their children with refinement, and to keep their own and their children's language pure and clean, very naturally are jealous of the influence of the magazine—especially of the *Century Magazine*—in this respect. Here is really a predicament, and feeling the predicament, we think at least a dialect story . . . where 'yup' is used for yes, for instance, and where all sorts of vulgarisms occur,—should very strongly recommend itself before being sent into almost every cultivated household in the U.S.!"[36]

Mark Twain's *Tom Sawyer Abroad*

Dodge's handling of Twain's *Tom Sawyer Abroad* demonstrates how hard she had to work to make sure that a much-desired literary property would satisfy both her child audience and their anxious parents. In 1892 Mark Twain had been approached by Dodge through a letter offering him $5,000 for serial rights to a boys' story of about 50,000 words. He wrote back declining the offer because he was busy with other things, but then an idea came to him for a series of stories describing the travels of Tom and Huck around the world, perhaps to be called "Huckleberry Finn and Tom Sawyer Abroad." When he had written about half of the first story, he told his publisher, Fred J. Hall, "I have written 26,000 words of it—and can add a million if required, by adding 'Africa,' 'England' 'Germany,' etc [sic] to the title page of each successive volume of the series." Twain believed his projected book would appeal to a wide audience. He said, "I conceive that the right way to write a story for boys is to write so that it will not only interest boys but will also strongly interest any man *who has ever been a boy*. That immensely *enlarges the audience*." Because of this approach to the story, he thought *Tom Sawyer Abroad* was as suitable for publication in an adult periodical as in a juvenile one, and told Hall so. Because Twain needed money badly at the time and because he felt Dodge's proposed 50,000 words might cramp his style, he set to work to place the book with another publisher. He held on, however, to the possibility of closing with Dodge and perhaps cutting the story off at some appropriate place so that he could pick it up elsewhere later.[37]

In 1890 Twain's family had rented a cottage at Onteora near Dodge's summer home, and the acquaintance between the two families deepened at this time into a lasting friendship (Wright 1979, 181). Dodge was especially close to Twain's daughters, and their father confided to Fred Hall that his family was *"strenuous"* that this first volume should appear in *St. Nicholas* and admitted, "Well, I should prefer that too." It was the price, though, that he found "just a considerable trifle moderate" after hearing that *Harper's* was paying Charles Dudley Warner $100 per 1,000 words.[38] When he was ready to give in, Twain told Hall, "If Mrs. Dodge wants it, let her have it. It falls nearly 10,000 words short of what she wanted for $5000 but if she isn't willing to pay $5000, let her pay $4000." He added craftily, "It is finished and doesn't need another finish; but I have left it so that I can take it up again if required and carry it on."[39]

Dodge took great pains with the letter she sent on receiving the manuscript of *Tom Sawyer Abroad.* Here she expresses as much pleasure as any author could wish with the arrival of the precious document, yet she is also frank about the difficulty presented to *St. Nicholas*'s young subscribers by the story's inconclusive ending:

> The Trouble is its ending, or rather its no ending. If only you would give Somebody's ingenuity and masterly touch to the work of a few concluding lines or paragraphs that would round off the story so to speak.
>
> With a serial, readers are more clamorous for some sort of definite ending than in the case of a book; and young folks, you know, are particularly exasperating in this respect. Of course no one could ask you to finish Tom Sawyer—that would be murder! But would it not be practicable to "satisfactorize" the present conclusion, say by a few paragraphs that would at least lure the fascinated reader into the belief that he had it all? Or perhaps it could so be done by a few touches that one would be satisfied to finish the story in one's own imagination.[40]

Dodge's draft of this letter, held in the Wilkinson Collection at Princeton, goes so far as to suggest the very dialogue that might be used to conclude the novel. But Twain promised Dodge he would come up with something better, and he did. The ending he devised for *St. Nicholas* satisfied Twain even better than his first effort, for he retained it when he published the story separately.

Twain, understanding the special demands of the *St. Nicholas* audience, said that when writing *Tom Sawyer Abroad* he had "tried to leave the improprieties all out," and if he didn't, "Mrs. Dodge can scissor them out."[41] Dodge, for her part, promised to use the scissors "very sparingly and with a reverent hand"[42] but nonetheless cut approximately 2,000 words of Twain's text.[43]

O. M. Brack, author of an article on Dodge's "expurgation" of *Tom Sawyer Abroad*, [44] and Terry Firkins, editor of the novel for the California edition of the *Works*, see Dodge as having committed literary "mayhem" on Twain's text (Firkins, 248). It is thus worth looking closely at the changes she made in order to understand why she felt them necessary. Some of these alterations are directed toward tightening up loosely or carelessly written sentences. (Twain, desperate for money, wrote the 40,000-word story in a month.) But many more involve efforts to tone down Twain's use of dialect and to eliminate other "improprieties." In making such changes, Dodge was doing very much what Gilder and his staff did at the *Century*, where Twain's *Huckleberry Finn* "was blue-penciled not merely for egregiously coarse words or sentences but for whole passages depicting the routine cruelty and viciousness of midwestern villages" (John, 156).

Dodge made many minor verbal changes throughout the text, eliminating expressions she and her staff thought crude or offensive. As in the case of the Trowbridge story, some expressions are eliminated in one place and allowed to stand in another, the aim being not to purge the text of offensive material but to "tone down" the overall effect of the regional speech represented there. Tom and Huck emerge sounding just a bit more educated and proper in Dodge's version than in Twain's.

Sweating was apparently as unpardonable a vulgarity by *St. Nicholas*'s standards as it was by the *Century*'s (John, 155), and Dodge in her revisions allows no one in the story to "sweat"—even metaphorically. Colorful slang and graphic references to illness or bodily functions are also deleted regularly. Moreover, the effort to eliminate offensive detail was even carried over to the illustrations. Dan Beard, who illustrated *Tom Sawyer Abroad*, was told by Dodge that bare feet were vulgar, even for Tom and Huck, and in Beard's pictures both are neatly shod.[45]

O. M. Brack speaks of Dodge's attitudes toward what children should know as being "in the puritanical tradition" (Brack, 146) and claims that her editorial cuts show she wanted children "to be ignorant about alcohol" (Brack, 148). She does eliminate the drunkenness of the villagers in the first paragraph of the story and cuts Huck's comment that a character who is staggering about taking swigs from a bottle is drunk, though she retains Huck's observation in a later chapter that watching some whirling dervishes made *him* feel drunk. Dodge, who called alcoholism a "disease" and supported the work of the New York Inebriate Asylum to cure its victims,[46] did not ban mention of alcohol in *St. Nicholas* and was quite capable of allowing a humorous reference to it in her own "Letter-Box" department.[47] Her policy of preferring to treat drunkenness by indirect reference rather than direct description is quite like that of the *Century* (John, 155).

Brack and Firkins both comment on Dodge's excision of references to death and her minimizing of those references she could not avoid, making much of the fact that in one passage a bird is "not even allowed to sing on a dead limb" (Firkins, 249). But that limb is a small detail in a passage Dodge does not cut, one dealing quite vividly with the bird's death. One set of passages Dodge does cut involves an extended and graphic depiction of dead human bodies, described in pathetic and grotesque detail. Although death was not banned from *St. Nicholas*, it, like other harsh realities, was not dwelt on overlong.

Brack and Firkins stress the care with which Dodge eliminated slurs against religious groups. And it is true that she was careful "to avoid everything that tends to provoke religious controversy" ("Memoranda"). But there is a larger significance to many of these cuts which Brack and Firkins miss. A long passage Dodge omits on the art of "cussing" as practiced by bishops and popes in the Middle Ages is also a powerful indictment of medieval society's inhumanity, a sardonic set piece that compares favorably with Twain's best work, and Dodge's cutting of it may also have reflected her unwillingness to present to her readers so dark and effectively pessimistic a picture of human nature. Further, when Dodge eliminated a number of references that, taken together, create a mocking equation of Christian and Islamic religious beliefs and practices with lies and fairy tales, her changes substantially alter the tone and meaning of the story, making it much less satiric, less bleak in its view of human folly and wickedness.

Of course, as Clarke noted to Trowbridge, the editors at *St.*

Nicholas appreciated that things they might wish to delete for their own audience would be unobjectionable in a version published for older readers. And they were accustomed to giving warm notices to books they had cut when those books were later published in full. Unfortunately, in the case of *Tom Sawyer Abroad*, Twain's American publishers, under pressure to produce the book on time, set all but the last four chapters using the *St. Nicholas* version as copy text (Firkins, 624). Consequently, with the exception of those last chapters the book appeared in America as Dodge had modified it, and this first American edition, widely reprinted through the years, has been the version most American readers have encountered, a situation neither Twain nor Dodge could have predicted or would have wished.

Dodge, who was not the puritanical provider of literary "pabulum" (Brack, 146) envisioned by Brack and Firkins, went out of her way to find powerful, engaging work for her young readers, even when doing so meant including pieces that did not meet her stylistic norms or that might seem to some adult readers disturbing or in doubtful taste. Dodge's strategy for including such material involved a degree of editorial intervention that to a modern sensibility can seem unwarranted and intrusive. But as we have seen here, her conception of the editorial role involved a high degree of interaction with her contributors at every stage of their work. In accepting problematic work for publication in *St. Nicholas*, Dodge was willing to risk modifying the landscape of her pleasure garden, but she wished on the whole to keep it a safe space where "toads hop quickly out of sight and snakes dare not show themselves at all" ("CM," 354).

Dodge's Legacy

Unlike her friend and mentor Horace Scudder, Mary Mapes Dodge did not leave behind an array of books and articles outlining her ideas about children and their literature. Her literary testament is to be found in her correspondence, in the archival records of her editorial work—and in the magazine itself, for the perennial question "Is it right for *St. Nick?*" was, in the years 1873 to 1905, a question essentially to be decided by the architect of the "pleasure-ground" herself. The magazine, called into being by Dodge's vision, reflected her priorities, her taste.

As we have shown here, Dodge was more than just a figurehead; she was the guiding spirit of the whole enterprise. Although she was blessed with "appreciative, generous and helpful publishers" and "a staff of capable, tireless assistants," it was her "exceptional temperament," "unwearying application," and dedication to the task at hand that made her magazine unique. Hers were "the planning, inventing, inspiring, the new thought, the fresh combination, the motive and impulse" that were the "breath of its life." What we have examined in this chapter is what one of Dodge's closest friends described as the "incessant and absorbing labor"— "the enormous correspondence, the endless detail, the suggestion here, the alteration there" (Runkle, 287)—that went to make *St. Nicholas* "the best child's periodical in the world" (Whittier, 3).

9

Conclusion

Mary Mapes Dodge's *Hans Brinker* is an acknowledged classic of children's literature. And it is this durable best-seller of 1865 for which she is probably most remembered today. In Dodge's own time her lively essays and amusing light verse appeared in some of America's premier magazines. Her serious poems touched many contemporary readers as an apt expression of their own deepest concerns. And she was revered and loved by three generations of children as the peerless "Conductor" of *St. Nicholas* magazine. Dodge's conception of what the readers of *St. Nicholas* needed and wanted was a major influence on the development of American children's literature in what has justly been called a golden age. The roll call of distinguished authors she persuaded to write for children is impressive, and she had a gift for recognizing and encouraging fledgling talent. Her correspondence reveals the extent to which famous writers like Alcott, Twain, and Kipling deferred to her special knowledge of her audience and to her editorial expertise. It shows the gratitude of young writers like John Bennett, as well as the cordial respect of distinguished figures like Longfellow and Whittier. And a study of manuscripts and interoffice memorandums shows how deftly Dodge and her staff solicited and shaped work they published to fit her idea of what was "right for *St. Nick*."

Our inquiry into Dodge's personal history has explored the way her mission to children grew out of her own unusual schooling at home and her attempt to provide her sons with a similarly rich experience. For them Dodge created an ambience in which play was indistinguishable from education. The boys were encouraged to observe, experiment, research, and share their findings with an appreciative mother-teacher. Attentive to her sons' real likes and dislikes, Dodge discussed art and literature with them seriously and learned to respect the honesty and shrewdness of their responses. This lesson was to stand her in good stead in both her writing and her editorial work for children.

The pages of the *United States Journal*, which Dodge edited from 1861 to 1862, demonstrate that from the very beginning of her career she possessed the ability to project a strong and pleasing editorial personality. Her commitment to knowing and serving her audience was expressed in an immediate editorial call for reader participation in shaping the magazine's policies. In the *Journal* she began to write about many subjects that were to preoccupy her throughout her career. She discussed children and their upbringing, the function of play in education, and the value of an active outdoor life for young girls. She wrote thoughtfully and wittily about women's rights and about marriage, and included short profiles of women of achievement who might serve as role models for young girls. She experimented with popular formula fiction and directed the attention of her family audience to the way games, amusements, reading, and art might enrich their lives.

Dodge's *The Irvington Stories* (1864) is a kind of literary sampler, demonstrating her skill at writing many kinds of short fiction for children. Those stories which are most fully imagined show life from a child's perspective and are far more successful than those which invite the reader to identify emotionally with an adult narrator. When Dodge's imaginative empathy with children was completely engaged, her narrative voice was sure, controlled, effective; when she solicited an easy sentimental response from the reader, the result was often a serious failure of tone. "The Hermit of the Hills" treats a central theme in Dodge's work, concern with a troubled, divided family that must be restored to its original

unity through the efforts of its youngest members. The story is
also an early expression of Dodge's interest in themes of carnival
and festivity centering on Christmas. It is, however, marred by a
mawkish sentimentality common in magazine fiction of the time.
A much stronger story in the collection is "Captain George, the
Drummer-Boy," a surprisingly complex piece about the Civil War,
written while the war was still going on. Dodge appears to have
been asked to write a simple patriotic tale, but her empathy with
a young boy ill prepared for the realities of battle makes it a
bittersweet story, full of moral ambiguity and disillusion. General
George McClellan praised the story's honest picture of war, and
it deserves to be more widely read.

In *Hans Brinker* (1865) Dodge again presented realistically observed young people faced with problems readers could recognize
as not unlike their own. In this novel the adolescent quest for
identity and independence is shown to be difficult but rewarding.
The colorful Dutch setting is more than an appealing backdrop:
Dodge's vision of Holland as the "land of pluck" provides a rich
symbolic context suggesting what courage and endurance can do
for the weak and oppressed. With considerable skill, she created
a narrative structure for this story that could accommodate the
needs of a variety of readers. Her clever use of the story of the
"hero of Haarlem" to bring home a moral lesson to her youngest
readers made the story of the little boy who saved Holland part
of popular nursery mythology. Though, as noted in chapter 4, it
was not an original story, the little fable was well adapted to
instill in young readers an aspiration toward the virtues of self-
reliance, duty, honor, and hard work so admired in the genteel
tradition.

Dodge set her second novel, *Donald and Dorothy* (1883), in an
upper-middle-class American home full of books, pictures, opportunities for play, learning, and social interaction—the sort of
home where the *Century* and *St. Nicholas* might well be found.
The novel celebrates the educational effectiveness of such a setting in forming character, as the young protagonists bravely con-
front and defeat the representative of a slack and careless way of
life. But Dodge's honest depiction of the way her intelligent and

forthright heroine is diminished and frustrated by the ideal of womanhood presented to her in that very enlightened home complicates the story and qualifies the happy ending. The novel was popular in its day and remains interesting for its picture of genteel domestic life in the 1880s.

By the end of her long career as an editor, Dodge could look back on accomplishments that would, had her audience been primarily adult, have made her as widely recognized a shaper of intellectual history as any of her colleagues at the *Century*, *Harper's*, or the *Atlantic Monthly*. She herself had pointed out to Roswell Smith in her famous letter of 1873 that "the perfect magazine for children lies folded at the heart of the ideal best magazine for grown-ups," though the child's magazine had to be, if anything, "stronger, truer, bolder, more uncompromising" ("CM," 353). Dodge's editorial goals were not, in fact, so very different from those of Holland, Gilder, and Smith. *St. Nicholas* and the *Century* shared more than their offices and printing facilities; they shared a cultural, social, and political program.

Like *Scribner's Monthly* and the *Century*, *St. Nicholas* preached self-reliance, hard work, courage, duty, patriotism, and trust in God. And like its sister periodicals, *St. Nicholas* was reformist in its way. Young readers were reminded from time to time that poverty, disease, and homelessness afflicted innocents no older than they. And they were frequently urged to think of themselves as empowered to change the world for the better, and reminded that the future was theirs to shape. The world that children were shown in *St. Nicholas*—for the most part unrealistically safe and pretty—reflected some "harsh, cruel facts" and an "occasional glimpse of the odious doings of the uncharitable and base,"—when Dodge thought it important to point these out ("CM," 354). Of course, a serious limitation of *St. Nicholas* (and of *Scribner's Monthly* and the *Century*) was an uncritical equation of contemporary middle-class American values and assumptions with eternal verities. Looked at a century later, many of the "facts" uncritically acknowledged in its fiction are seen to be harsher and more cruel than they were ever judged to be in the text. Ethnic and racial minorities, for example, were often depicted stereotypically, in painful and degrading terms. Though Dodge did become more sensitive to this issue as time went on, many pages of the magazine during her tenure as editor are marred by an acceptance of the racism, sexism, and ethnic and class prejudice characteristic of her milieu.

Dodge was aware of her own fallibility as an editor. *St. Nicholas* was often praised in extravagant terms, but such flattery made her uneasy, and her correspondence shows that she was often less than satisfied with what she had been able to produce, even when it was well received by the public and the critics. Dodge had said at the outset of her career that it was a heavy responsibility to have the ear of young America once a month, and part of this responsibility lay in maintaining consistently high standards. She frequently complained of the "trials and disappointments" of being an editor: "fair ideals" she lamented, "get so woefully squeezed under printing and binding presses!"[1] And it was a strain to be personally responsible for keeping a magazine up to the mark. She once told the editor of the *Atlantic Monthly* that she'd often "noticed that the more 'new life' there is in a magazine the less there is left in its editor!"[2]

An especially pressing editorial burden was the constant need to accommodate the demands of a divided audience. Adults often saw *St. Nicholas* as a convenient vehicle for inculcating the values of the genteel tradition. Dodge, on the other hand, perceived children as wanting "to have their own way over their own magazine" ("CM," 353). Her readiness to listen to her young readers, her respect for their views, her orientation toward the future, and her openness to experiment allied her with forces that were changing the very nature of children's literature in her time; even so, she never forgot that she had to please not only the children but their parents. She worked tirelessly to balance the needs of her various constituencies and to meet the demands of her own taste and conscience.

The volumes of *St. Nicholas* published under her direction from 1873 to 1905 prove how well, on balance, she was able to do just that. The editor of a literary periodical needs the ability to attract and keep an effective staff; a flair for business; a sense of audience;

the ability to find and cultivate different kinds of contributors; and the skill to select, modify, and arrange materials effectively. Dodge had all of these. The program that gave *St. Nicholas* its direction reflected her long-term commitment to bringing enlightenment, entertainment, and cultural enrichment to American families. But as Dodge rightly observed, no program, however well devised, can quite make a magazine. It takes something more—an individual vision, a personality whose taste and enthusiasm can give the project life. As we have suggested, Dodge's concept of *St. Nicholas* as a "pleasure-ground" for children had its sources in her experience as a mother, a journalist, a writer of fiction, a lover of games and festivity. In the holiday spirit invoked by its very name, in its earnest but unpreachy morality, in its openness to new things, and in its humor and playfulness *St. Nicholas* reflected its editor's own approach to life. It achieved, brilliantly, her goal—to bring children the very best in literature and art. And it was fun. In Mary Mapes Dodge's "pleasure-ground" the "first culture of the mind" ("Kindergarten," 258) was attended with delight.

Notes and References

Permission has been given to publish from the following sources:

Century Company Archives, New York Public Library, cited as C: NYPL.

Donald and Robert M. Dodge Collection, Princeton University Library, cited as P: DRMD.

Horace Scudder Papers, the Huntington Library, cited as HL.

Mary Mapes Dodge Letters, Houghton Library, Harvard University, cited as H.

Mary Mapes Dodge Collection, Princeton University Library, cited as P: MMD.

Mary Mapes Dodge Letters, University of Virginia Library, cited as UVL.

Scribner Archives, Princeton University Library, cited as P:S.

Wilkinson Collection, Princeton University Library, cited as P:W.

William Fayal Clarke letter, Beinecke Library, Yale University, cited as B.

Preface

1. *Hans Brinker; or, The Silver Skates* (New York: James O'Kane, 1865); *Hans Brinker; or, The Silver Skates: A Story of Life in Holland*, revised ed. with introduction by the author (New York: Charles Scribner's Sons, 1873); hereafter cited in text as *HB*.

2. Until July 1881, the magazine's full title was *St. Nicholas: Scribner's Illustrated Magazine for Girls and Boys*; for the rest of Dodge's editorship, it was titled *St. Nicholas: An Illustrated Magazine for Young Folks*. For convenience in this volume the magazine will be referred to as *St. Nicholas* in text and cited in Notes and References as *SN*.

3. "Children's Magazines," *Scribner's Monthly*, 6 July 1873, 354; hereafter cited in text as "CM."

4. Catharine Morris Wright, *Lady of the Silver Skates: The Life and Letters of Mary Mapes Dodge* (Jamestown, R.I.: Clingstone Press, 1979); hereafter cited in text.

5. *The Irvington Stories* (New York: J. O'Kane, 1865); *The Irvington*

Stories, revised and enlarged by the author (New York: William L. Allison 1898; Chicago: M. A. Donahue, 1898); hereafter cited in text as *IS*.

6. *Donald and Dorothy* (Boston: Roberts Brothers, 1883; New York: Century Company, 1899); hereafter cited in text as *DD*. All references will be to the 1899 edition.

7. Jerome Griswold, *"Hans Brinker*: Sunny World, Angry Waters," *Children's Literature* 12 (1984): 47–60; hereafter cited in text.

8. "The Little Dutch Hero," *Boy's Own Magazine*, 1855, 292; hereafter cited in text as "Dutch Hero."

9. "The Little Dykeman," *Old Merry's Annual* (1871), 638–40; hereafter cited in text as "Dykeman."

10. *A Few Friends and How They Amused Themselves: A Tale in Nine Chapters Containing Descriptions of Twenty Pastimes and Games, and a Fancy Dress Party* (Philadelphia: Lippincott, 1869); hereafter cited in text as *FF*.

11. R. Gordon Kelly, *Mother Was a Lady: Self and Society in Selected American Children's Periodicals, 1865–1890* (Westport, Conn.: Greenwood Press, 1974); hereafter cited in text.

12. R. Gorden Kelly, ed., *Children's Periodicals of the United States* (Westport, Conn.: Greenwood Press, 1984); hereafter cited in text.

13. Fred Erisman, "St. Nicholas," in Kelly 1984; hereafter cited in text.

14. Fred Erisman, "There Was a Child Went Forth: A Study of *St. Nicholas Magazine* and Selected Children's Authors, 1890–1915," diss. (Ann Arbor, Mich.: University Microfilms, 1966).

15. Mary June Roggenbuck, "*St. Nicholas Magazine:* A Study of the Impact and Historical Influence of the Editorship of Mary Mapes Dodge," diss. (Ann Arbor, Mich.: University Microfilms, 1976).

16. Lawrence Fuller, "Mary Mapes Dodge and *St. Nicholas*: The Development of a Philosophy and Practice of Publishing for Young People," paper presented at the annual meeting of the National Council of Teachers of English, Detroit, Michigan, November 1984 (ERIC Educational Document Reproduction Service, November 1984, ED 251 847).

17. Catharine Morris Wright, "How 'St. Nicholas' Got Rudyard Kipling: And What Happened Then," *Princeton University Library Chronicle* 35 (Spring 1974): 259–89; hereafter cited in text.

18. Kate Douglas Wiggin, *Polly Oliver's Problem*, serialized in *SN* November 1892–May 1893, 6–14, 97–105, 198–207, 297–306, 346–51, 420–26, 502–8.

19. John Townsend Trowbridge, *His One Fault* (Boston: Lee & Shepard Publishers; New York: Charles T. Dillingham, 1887); serialized in *SN*, November 1884–October 1885, 4–10, 133–35, 189–91, 272–78, 413–18, 501–7, 590–96, 669–75, 767–71, 821–26, 905–9; hereafter cited in text.

Chapter One

1. William Fayal Clarke, "In Memory of Mary Mapes Dodge," *SN*, October 1905, 1065; hereafter cited in text.
2. Leroy Fairman, quoted in Fayal Clarke, "Fifty Years of St. Nicholas: A Brief Anniversary Compilation of Chronicle and Comment," *SN* November 1923, 20; hereafter cited in text.
3. Although most sources give the date of Dodge's birth as 1831, Catharine Morris Wright, in her biography authorized by the Dodge family, suggests that the year was 1830. While it is true that in the last year of her life Dodge wrote a poem titled "1905 Seventy-five," which Wright reprints (Wright 1979, 227–28), the memorial piece published in *St. Nicholas* by William Fayal Clarke at Dodge's death gives her year of birth as 1831 (Clarke 1905, 1060). And Clarke was not only her colleague but a member of her household for many years. Jeannette Gilder who as a girl knew Dodge's family well, agrees with Clarke in giving Dodge's age at death as 74 ("The Newark Life of Mary Mapes Dodge," *Critic* 47, no. 4 [October 1905] :292), the age also listed in the records at the Evergreen Cemetery in Hillside, New Jersey.
4. Lucia Gilbert Runkle, "Mary Mapes Dodge," in *Our Famous Women. Comprising the Lives and Deeds of American Women Who Have Distinguished Themselves in Literature, Science, Art, Music, and the Drama, or Are Famous as Heroines, Patriots, Orators, Educators, Physicians, Philanthropists, etc. With Numerous Anecdotes, Incidents, and Personal Experiences* (Hartford, Conn.: A.D. Worthington, 1884), 277; hereafter cited in text.
5. "Personal" ad, *New York Times*, 6 November 1858, quoted in Wright 1979, 15.
6. Robert Dale Owen to Dodge, 10 August 1867, PU:W.
7. Mapes to Dodge, 14 May 1864, printed in Wright 1979, 25.
8. John L. Motley, *The Rise of the Dutch Republic*, 3 vols. (New York: F. Warne, 1855).
9. John L. Motley, *The History of the United Netherlands*, 4 vols. (New York: Harper & Brothers, 1864–68).
10. Review of *Hans Brinker*, *Harper's New Monthly Magazine*, March 1866, 526, quoted in Richard Darling, *The Rise of Children's Book Reviewing in America, 1865–1881* (New York: R. R. Bowker, 1968), 229; hereafter cited in text.
11. Review of *Hans Brinker*, *Nation*, 25 January 1866, 119–20, quoted in Darling 1968, 229–30.
12. *Philadelphia Inquirer*, quoted in "Opinions of the American Press," advertising supplement bound in *SN*, January 1875, 4.
13. *Rhymes and Jingles* (New York: Scribner, Armstrong, 1875); hereafter cited in text as *RJ*.

•

14. *Theophilus and Others* (New York: Scribner, Armstrong, 1876); hereafter cited in text as *TO*.

15. Charles Mapes to Catherine T. Bunnell, n.d., quoted in Wright 1979, 98.

16. *Along the Way* (New York: Charles Scribner's Sons, 1879); hereafter cited in text as *AW*.

17. Dodge to James Dodge, 30 March 1880, quoted in Wright 1979, 118.

18. Dodge to Bunnell, 27 July 1880, quoted in Wright 1979, 119.

19. Dodge to James Dodge, 30 March 1880, quoted in Wright 1979, 118.

20. Dodge to Bunnell, 27 July 1880, quoted in Wright 1979, 118.

21. "Funeral Notice," quoted in Wright 1979, 120.

22. Dodge to Bunnell, 1 June 1881, quoted in Wright 1979, 123.

23. Elizabeth Stuart Phelps, "Supporting Herself," *SN*, May 1884, 517.

24. Annie Nathan Meyer, *Barnard Beginnings* (Boston: Houghton Mifflin, 1935), 48; hereafter cited in text.

25. Dodge to [Lucy] Morse, 28 January 1886, quoted in Wright 1979, 154.

26. Candace Wheeler, *Yesterdays in a Busy Life* (New York: Harper & Brothers, 1918), 288.

27. Sarah S. McEnery, "Mary Mapes Dodge: An Intimate Tribute," *Critic* 47, no. 4 (October 1905): 311.

28. *The Land of Pluck: Stories and Sketches for Young Folk* (New York: Century, 1894).

29. *When Life Is Young: A Collection of Verse for Boys and Girls* (New York: Century, 1894); hereafter cited in text as *LY*.

30. *A New Baby World: Stories, Rhymes, and Pictures for Little Folks Compiled from "St. Nicholas"* (New York: Century, 1897).

31. *The Children's Book of Recitations* (New York: DeWitt Publishing House, 1898).

32. *The Irvington Stories*, new edition, revised and enlarged by the author (New York: William L. Allison, 1898).

33. *Rhymes and Jingles*, enlarged edition, illustrated by Sarah S. Stillwell (New York: Scribner, 1904).

34. *Poems and Verses* (New York: Century, 1879); hereafter cited in text as *PV*.

35. Records at the Evergreen Cemetery in Hillside, New Jersey, where she was buried, list the cause of death as cancer of the liver.

Chapter Two

1. "The Book Table," *Working Farmer*, January 1861, 19.
2. "The Book Table," *Working Farmer*, May 1861, 114.
3. "The Book Table," *Working Farmer*, April 1861, 77.
4. "Seasonable Recipes," *Working Farmer*, August 1861, 189.
5. Letter to the editor, *Working Farmer and United States Journal*, January 1862 5; hereafter this periodical will be cited in Notes and References as *WF&USJ*.
6. "To Our Readers," *WF&USJ*, November 1861, 256; hereafter cited in text as "Readers."
7. "Kindergarten," *WF&USJ* November 1861, 258; hereafter cited in text as "Kindergarten."
8. "Blue Laws of Connecticut," *WF&USJ*, November 1861, 259.
9. Review of Caroline Dall, *Women's Rights under the Law*, *WF&USJ*, December 1861, 281.
10. "Pocket Money," *WF&USJ*, December 1861, 281.
11. "What Are the Girls About?" *WF&USJ*, March 1862, 64.
12. "Le Longue Carbine; or, The Borderer's Dream," *WF&USJ*, December 1861, 256–58.
13. "Gaston Glencoe; an Incident in the Siege of Fort Meigs," *WF&USJ*, December 1861, 279–80.
14. *WF&USJ* April 1862, 86–88.
15. "Shoddy," *WF&USJ*, April 1862, 89.
16. "Shoddy Aristocracy in America," *Cornhill Magazine*, May 1865, 43–59.
17. "The Rights of the Body," *WF&USJ*, January 1862, 18.
18. Dodge to Scudder, 23 July 1866, HN.
19. Dodge to Scudder, 23 July 1866, HN.
20. "The Funny Land of Pluck," *Riverside Magazine for Young People*, May 1867, 230–34; June 1867, 275–78.
21. Dodge to Scudder, 23 January 1867, HN.
22. "The Land of Pluck," *Riverside Magazine for Young People*, September 1867, 397–401.
23. "Holiday Whispers concerning Games and Toys," *Riverside Magazine for Young People*, January 1868, 41–44; hereafter cited in text as "Holiday Whispers."
24. "Kaleidoscopes and Burglars," *Riverside Magazine for Young People*, February 1868, 76–80.
25. "Bessie's Birthday Party," *Riverside Magazine for Young People*, April 1868, 178–83.
26. "Croquet at Midnight," *Riverside Magazine for Young People*, October 1868, 451–53; November 1868, 514–19.

27. "A Midnight Visit to Clio," *Riverside Magazine for Young People*, December 1868, 564–66.

28. Dodge to Scudder, 12 November 1868, HN.

29. Advertising notice, *Hearth and Home*, 18 January 1875, 45.

30. Dodge to [James H.] Bates, 27 September 1869, printed in Wright 1979, 58.

31. Dodge to Bunnell, 3 April 1893, quoted in Wright 1979, 71.

32. Dodge to Seymour, 14 May 1876, quoted in Wright 1979, 95–96.

33. Dodge to Seymour, n.d., printed in Wright 1979, 96.

34. "Culture and Progress," *Scribner's Monthly*, November 1876, 36.

35. Julia R. Tutwiler, "Mary Mapes Dodge in New York City," in *Women Authors of Our Day in Their Homes: Personal Descriptions and Interviews*, edited with additions by Francis Whiting Halsey (New York: James Pott, 1903), 260; hereafter cited in text.

36. See, for example, *HB*, chap. 23.

37. Rusticus Gent [Garrit Furman], "Cain," in *Long Island Miscellanies* (New York: Egbert, Hovey & King, 1847), 68–72.

38. "Culture and Progress," *Scribner's Monthly*, November 1876, 36.

Chapter Three

1. Review, *Working Farmer*, December 1864, 258.

2. Dodge to Charles Scribner, 29 June 1891, PU:S.

3. Alexander Medlicott, Jr., " 'For the Instruction of the Young': The Deerfield Captivity Narratives," *Children's Literature* 12 (1984): 26; hereafter cited in text.

Chapter Four

1. Because of the number of editions of *Hans Brinker* that are available, all subsequent citations will refer to chapters rather than pages.

2. Review of *Hans Brinker*, *Nation*, 25 January 1866, 119–20, quoted in Darling 1968, 229–30.

3. Review of *Hans Brinker*, *Atlantic Monthly*, July 1866, 779–80, quoted in Darling 1968, 231.

4. Review of *Hans Brinker*, *Independent*, 19 April 1866, 3, quoted in Darling 1968, 230.

5. Review of *Hans Brinker*, *Atlantic Monthly*, July 1899, 780, quoted in Darling 1968, 232.

6. Review of *Hans Brinker*, *Scribner's Monthly*, February 1874, 504, quoted in Darling 1968, 234.

7. Marilyn Kaye, afterword to *Hans Brinker; or, The Silver Skates: A Story of Life in Holland*, Signet Classic ed. (New York: New American Library, 1986), 299; hereafter cited in text.

8. Harriet Christy, "Mary Mapes Dodge," in *Writers for Children: Critical Studies of the Major Authors since the Seventeenth Century*, ed. Jane Bingham (New York: Charles Scribner's Sons, 1988), 195; hereafter cited in text.

9. Mikhail Bakhtin, *Theory and History of Literature*, vol 8 of *Problems of Dostoevsky's Poetics*, ed. and trans. Caryl Emerson (Minneapolis: University of Minnesota Press, 1984), 8:122; hereafter cited in text.

10. Sanjay Sircar, "The Victorian Auntly Narrative Voice and Mrs. Molesworth's *Cuckoo Clock*," *Children's Literature* 17 (1989):1–24.

11. Dodge to Mr. [Edward] Seymour, 13 October 1873, P:S.

12. Walter J. Ong, *Orality and Literacy: The Technologizing of the Word* (London: Methuen, 1982), 141; hereafter cited in text.

Chapter Five

1. Jerome Bruner, *On Knowing: Essays for the Left Hand*, expanded ed. (Cambridge, Mass.: Belknap Press of Harvard University Press, 1979), 1; hereafter cited in text.

2. Madeleine Stern, "Louisa Alcott's Self-Criticism," in *Studies in the American Renaissance: 1988*, ed. Joel Myerson (Charlottesville: University Press of Virginia, 1988), 339; hereafter cited in text.

3. Dodge to Longfellow, 25 May 1877, HL.

4. "Letter-Box," *SN*, December 1974, 125.

5. Russel Nye, *The Unembarrassed Muse: The Popular Arts in America* (New York: Dial Press, 1970), 94; hereafter cited in text.

6. George B. Cheever, preface, to *American Common-Place Book of Poetry* (1831), quoted in Nye, 94.

7. Review of *Rhymes and Jingles, Harper's New Monthly Magazine*, quoted in Marilyn Karrenbrock, "Mary Mapes Dodge," in *Dictionary of Literary Biography* (Detroit: Gale, 1985), 42: 156; hereafter cited in text.

8. *Nation*, quoted in Karrenbrock, 42:156.

9. Edmund C. Stedman, *Poets of America* (Cambridge, Mass.: Riverside Press, 1885), 1:446.

Chapter Six

1. "Letter-Box," *SN*, April 1883, 476.

2. "Letter-Box," *SN*, February 1883, 317.

3. "Letter-Box," *SN*, April 1883, 476.

4. "Letter-Box," *SN*, December 1882, 156.

5. "Recent Fiction," *Century*, August 1885, 651.

6. John Cawelti, *Adventure, Mystery, and Romance* (Chicago: University of Chicago Press, 1976), 46; hereafter cited in text.

7. Nina Baym, *Women's Fiction: A Guide to Novels by and about Women in America, 1820–1870* (Ithaca, N.Y.: Cornell University Press, 1978), 35; hereafter cited in text.

8. Nancy K. Miller, "Emphasis Added: Plots and Plausibilities in Women's Fiction," in *The New Feminist Criticism: Essays on Women, Literature, and Theory*, ed. Elaine Showalter (New York: Pantheon, 1985), 347.

9. Barbara Welter, *Dimity Convictions: The American Woman in the Nineteenth Century* (Athens: Ohio University Press, 1976), 21.

10. Frances B. Cogan, *All-American Girl: The Ideal of Real Womanhood in Mid-Nineteenth-Century America* (Athens: University of Georgia Press, 1989), 4.

11. *Donald and Dorothy* (New York: Century, 1899).

12. Dodge to [Thomas] Niles, 1 August [1883], UVL.

13. Dodge to Niles, 28 January 1886, UVL.

Chapter Seven

1. [Josiah G. Holland] "Topics of the Time," *Scribner's Monthly*, November 1870, 106. Discussed also in Samuel C. Chew, ed., *Fruit among the Leaves: An Anniversary Anthology* (New York: Appleton-Century-Crofts, 1950), 77; hereafter cited in text.

2. Arthur John, *The Best Years of the "Century": Richard Watson Gilder, "Scribner's Monthly," and the "Century Magazine," 1870–1901* (Urbana: University of Illinois Press, 1981), 31; hereafter cited in text.

3. Quoted in Tutwiler, 262–63.

4. Leroy Fairman, quoted in Clarke 1923, 20.

5. [Hartford] *Times*; quoted in "Opinions of the American Press," advertising supplement bound in *SN*, January 1875, 4.

6. *Liberal Christian* (24 October 1874), quoted in "Opinions of the American Press," advertising supplement bound in *SN*, January 1875, 3.

7. *New York Tribune*, quoted in "Opinions of the American Press," advertising supplement bound in *SN*, January 1875, 4.

8. John G. Whittier, quoted in "What Some Eminent Men Think of St. Nicholas," Advertising supplement bound in *SN*, January 1875, 1; hereafter cited in text.

9. Charles Dudley Warner, quoted in "What Some Eminent Men Think of St. Nicholas," advertising supplement bound in *SN*, January 1875, 1.

10. Roswell Smith to Dodge, 1876, quoted in Wright 1979, 98–99.

11. Quoted in Tutwiler, 264.

12. Quoted in Tutwiler, 264.

13. For example, Dodge to Albert Bigelow Paine, 20 June 1900, HN.

14. For example, Dodge to Scudder, 23 August 1875, HN, or Dodge to Scudder, 11 July 1876, HN.

15. Quoted in Tutwiler, 265.

16. Dodge to Scudder, 22 September 1869, HN.

17. "Jack-in-the-Pulpit," *SN*, November 1875, 54.

18. "Jack-in-the-Pulpit," *SN*, November 1875, 54.

19. "Jack-in-the-Pulpit," *SN*, August 1875, 648–49.

20. Dodge to Scudder, 9 May 1867, HN.

21. *Springfield Republican*, quoted in "What the American Press Says of the Bound Volume," advertising supplement bound in *SN*, January 1875, 4. Samuel Griswold Goodrich (1793–1860) published phenomenally popular books and magazines for children under the pseudonym Peter Parley.

22. "Letter-Box," *SN*, January 1882, 260.

23. "Jack-in-the-Pulpit," *SN*, January 1874, 173.

24. "Letter-Box," *SN*, March 1876, 340.

25. Oliver Herford to Clarke, n.d. [1891], B.

26. Scudder to Dodge, 20 April 1867, PU:W.

27. Dodge to Charles Scribner, July 1877, P:S

28. Sarah Orne Jewett to Dodge, 7 December, P:W.

29. Lucius Aurelius Bigelow to Paine, 30 May 1901, HN.

30. David Macgregor Cheney to Paine, 6 December 1902, HN.

31. Cheney to Dodge, 2 May 1903, HN.

32. Among those who belonged to the league down through the years were Edna St. Vincent Millay, Alan Seeger, Robert Benchley, F. Scott Fitzgerald, Eudora Welty, Ring Lardner, Stephen Vincent Benét, Norman BelGeddes, Edmund Wilson, Elinor Wylie, William Faulkner, and E. B. White.

33. Dodge to Scudder, 23 August 1867, HN.

34. Dodge to Scudder, 23 January 1867, HN.

35. Dodge to Seymour, 14 July 1874, P:S.

Chapter Eight

1. Editors of Children's Monthly, "Prospectus," (New York: Scribner, 1873); hereafter cited in text as *P*. This item is on the reverse side of a note from Dodge to Scudder, 15 May 1873, HN.

2. Dodge to Scudder, 9 March 1885, HN.

3. Dodge to Scudder, 9 March 1885, HN.

4. Dodge to Scudder, 13 July 1868, HN.

5. Bennett to Spencer Mapes, 20 February 1937, PU: DRMD.

6. Whittier to Dodge, 24 September 1883, printed in Wright 1979, 137.

7. Longfellow to Dodge, 26 April 1877, printed in Wright 1979, 107.

8. Dodge to Gilder, April 1880, printed in Wright 1979, 117.

9. Alcott to Dodge, 10 September [1875], printed in *The Selected Letters of Louisa May Alcott*, ed. Joel Myerson and Daniel Shealy (Boston: Little, Brown, 1987), 195–96.

10. Dodge to Alcott, 22 January 1880, UV.

11. Dodge to Alcott, 15 March 1882, UV.

12. Dodge to Alcott, 12 January 1884, UV.

13. For example, Alcott to Dodge, 2 December [1874], printed in Stern, 368–69.

14. Dodge to Larcom, TS, 5 December 1874, PU:DRMD.

15. Dodge to Larcom, TS, 3 November 1875, PU:DRMD.

16. Dodge to Larcom, TS, 27 March 1876, PU:DRMD.

17. Dodge to Larcom, TS, 17 June 1876, PU:DRMD.

18. William Carey to Dodge, Sunday afternoon [14 February 1892], printed in Wright 1974, 264.

19. Kipling to Dodge, 21 February 1892, printed in Wright 1974, 265.

20. Kipling to Dodge, 8 October 1892, printed in Wright 1974, 270.

21. Kipling to Dodge, 15 October 1892, printed in Wright 1974, 272–73.

22. Draft letter, Dodge to Kipling, 19 October 1892, printed in Wright 1974, 275.

23. Kipling to Dodge, 29 October 1893, printed in Wright 1974, 286.

24. Dodge to Scudder, 12 August 1868, HN.

25. "Memoranda of Slight Changes That, from the *St. Nicholas* Point of View, Would Be Advisable in the MS. of 'Uncle Percy's Legends,'" enclosure in letter from William Fayal Clarke to E. H. House, 11 August 1898, UV; hereafter cited in text as "Memoranda."

26. Dodge to Scudder, 18 November 1866, HN.

27. Stedman to Dodge, 31 January 1893, PU:MMD.

28. Stevenson to Dodge, 5 April 1887, printed in Wright 1979, 157.

29. Custer to Dodge, n.d., PU:MMD.

30. Frank R. Stockton, quoted in Thomas Beer, *The Mauve Decade* (New York: Vintage Books, 1961), 161.

31. Notes enclosed in a letter from Chapin to Spencer Mapes, 11 September 1937, PU:DRMD.

32. Notes enclosed in a letter from Chapin to Spencer Mapes, 11 September 1937, PU:DRMD.

33. Dodge to Scudder, 7 November 1867, HN.

34. Elizabeth C. Saler and Edwin H. Cady, "The *St. Nicholas* and the Serious Artist," in *Essays Mostly on Periodical Publishing in America: A Collection in Honor of Clarence Gohdes*, ed. James Woodress with the assistance of Townsend Ludington and Joseph Arpad (Durham, N.C.: Duke University Press, 1973), 170; hereafter cited in text.

35. William Fayal Clarke, "Memoranda concerning *His One Fault*," Century Company Archives, New York Public Library, n.d.; hereafter cited in text.

36. Gilder, quoted in Herbert F. Smith, *Richard Watson Gilder* (New York: Twayne Publishers, 1970), 45.

37. Mark Twain to Fred J. Hall, 10 August 1892, printed in *Mark Twain's Letters to his Publishers, 1867–1894*, ed. Hamlin Hill (Berkeley and Los Angeles: University of California Press, 1967), 313–15; hereafter cited as Hill.

38. Twain to Hall, 10 August 1892, printed in Hill, 315.

39. Twain to Hall, 31 October 1892, printed in Hill, 324.

40. Dodge to Twain, 19 November 1892, printed in Wright 1979, 182–83.

41. Twain to Hall, 10 August 1892, printed in Hill, 324.

42. Dodge to Twain, 19 November 1892, printed in Wright 1979, 183.

43. Terry Firkins, "Textual Introduction," in Mark Twain, *Tom Sawyer; Tom Sawyer Abroad; Tom Sawyer, Detective*, vol. 4 of *The Works of Mark Twain*, ed. John C. Gerber, Paul Baender, and Terry Firkins (Berkeley and Los Angeles: University of California Press, 1980), 4:623, n. 3; hereafter cited in text.

44. O. M. Brack, Jr., "Mark Twain in Kneepants: The Expurgation of *Tom Sawyer Abroad*," in *Proof: The Yearbook of American Bibliographical and Texual Studies*, ed. Joseph Katz (Columbia: University of South Carolina Press, 1972), 2: 146; hereafter cited in text.

45. Cyril Clemens to Spencer Mapes, 6 January 1935, PU:W.

46. "Asylum for Inebriates," *WF&USJ*, February 1862, 38.

47. "Letter-Box," *SN*, November 1878, 69.

Chapter Nine

1. Dodge to Scudder, 4 December 1866, HN.

2. Dodge to Scudder, 9 September 1891, HN.

Selected Bibliography

Unpublished Library Holdings

Century Company Archives, New York Public Library.
Donald and Robert M. Dodge Collection, Princeton University Library.
Horace Scudder Papers, the Huntington Library.
Mary Mapes Dodge Letters, Houghton Library, Harvard University.
Mary Mapes Dodge Collection, Princeton University Library.
Mary Mapes Dodge Letters, University of Virginia Library.
Scribner Archives, Princeton University Library.
Wilkinson Collection. Princeton University Library.
William Fayal Clarke letter, Beinecke Library, Yale University.

Primary Sources

Fiction

Donald and Dorothy. Boston: Roberts Brothers, 1883. *A Few Friends and How They Amused Themselves: A Tale in Nine Chapters containing Descriptions of Twenty Pastimes and Games, and a Fancy-Dress Party*. Philadelphia: J. B. Lippincott, 1868.
Hans Brinker: or, The Silver Skates. New York: James O'Kane, 1865. Rev. with new preface as *Hans Brinker: or, The Silver Skates. A Story of Life in Holland*. Scribner, Armstrong, 1873.
The Irvington Stories. New York: James O'Kane, 1865. New ed., rev. and enl. New York: William L. Allison, 1898; Chicago: M. A. Donohue, 1898.

Editorial Work

Working Farmer and United States Journal. 1861–62.
St. Nicholas: Scribner's Illustrated Magazine for Boys and Girls.
     1873–81.
St. Nicholas: An Illustrated Magazine for Young Folks. 1881–1905.

Essays, Sketches, and Articles

"Bessie's Birthday Party." *Riverside Magazine for Young People,* April
     1868, 178–83.
"Children's Magazines." *Scribner's Monthly,* July 1873, 352–54.
"Croquet at Midnight; or, The Wonderful Secret." *Riverside Magazine for
     Young People,* October 1868, 451–53; November 1868, 514–19.
"A Day with Dr. Brooks." *Scribner's Monthly,* November 1870, 36–58.
"The Funny Land of Pluck." *Riverside Magazine for Young People,* May
     1867, 230–34:; June 1867, 275–78.
"Holiday Whispers concerning Toys and Games." *Riverside Magazine for
     Young People,* January 1869, 41–44.
"Kaleidoscopes and Burglars." *Riverside Magazine for Young People,* Feb-
     ruary 1868, 76–80.
"The Land of Pluck." *Riverside Magazine for Young People,* September
     1867, 397–401.
The Land of Pluck: Stories and Sketches for Young Folk. New York:
     Century, 1894.
"A Midnight Visit to Clio." *Riverside Magazine for Young People,* Decem-
     ber 1868, 564–66.
"Shoddy Aristocracy in America." *Cornhill,* May 1865, 43–59.
Theophilus and Others. New York: Scribner, Armstrong, 1876.

Poetry

Along the Way. New York: Charles Scribner's Sons, 1879.
Rhymes and Jingles. New York: Scribner, Armstrong, 1875. Enl. Ed. New
     York: Scribners, 1904.
When Life Is Young: A Collection of Verse for Boys and Girls. New York:
     Century, 1894.
Poems and Verses, New York, Century, 1904.

Compilations

Baby Days: A Selection of Songs, Stories, and Pictures, for Very Little Folks. New York: Scribner's, 1877.
Baby World: Stories, Rhymes, and Pictures for Little Folks: From St. Nicholas. New York: Century, 1884. Rev. as *A New Baby World: Stories, Rhymes, and Pictures for Little Folks.* New York: Century, 1897.
The Children's Book of Recitations. New York: DeWitt, 1898.

Secondary Sources

Books and Parts of Books

Alcott, Louisa May. *Selected Letters.* Edited by Joel Myerson and Daniel Shealy. Boston: Little, Brown, 1987. Useful for the letters that reflect the friendship and working relationship between Dodge and Alcott.
Brack, O. M., Jr. "Mark Twain in Knee Pants: The Expurgation of *Tom Sawyer Abroad.*" In *Proof: The Yearbook of American Bibliographical and Textual Studies*, vol. 2, edited by Joseph Katz. Columbia: University of South Carolina Press, 1972. Illustrates the problems of censorship imposed on Twain by the constraints of the genteel tradition when he published in *St. Nicholas.*
Burlingame, Roger. *Of Making Many Books: A Hundred Years of Reading, Writing, and Publishing.* New York: Charles Scribner's Sons, 1946. A valuable history of the house of Scribner, drawing on many personal reminiscences and letters.
Chew, Samuel B., ed. *Fruit among the Leaves: An Anniversary Anthology.* New York: Appleton-Century-Crofts, 1950. A history of the Century Company, particularly useful for its descriptions of the publishing world in New York in the late nineteenth century.
Commager, Henry Steele, ed. *A St. Nicholas Anthology.* New York: Random House, 1948. Valuable because it contains reprints of *St. Nicholas* not otherwise available.
Darling, Richard. *The Rise of Children's Book Reviewing in America. 1865–1881.* New York: R. R. Bowker, 1968. Useful for the samples of reviews presented, especially for the extensive study of the reviews of *Hans Brinker.*
Firkins, Terry, "Textual Introduction." In *Tom Sawyer: Tom Sawyer Abroad: Tom Sawyer. Detective*, vol. 4 of *The Works of Mark Twain*, edited by John C. Gerber, Paul Baender, and Terry Firkins. Berkeley

and Los Angeles: University of California Press, 1980. A study of the textual history of *Tom Sawyer Abroad*.

Griffin, Martin, *Frank R. Stockton*. Philadelphia: University of Pennsylvania Press, 1939. A comprehensive study of Dodge's close personal friend and first assistant editor at *St. Nicholas*.

Guthrie, Anna Lorraine, comp. *Index to St. Nicholas: Volumes 1–45, 1873–1918*. New York: H. W. Wilson, 1920. Essential for any analysis of the contributors and contents of *St. Nicholas*.

Howard, Alice B. *Mary Mapes Dodge of St. Nicholas*. New York: Messner, 1943. A fictionalized biography intended for a juvenile audience. Contains a number of inaccuracies.

John, Arthur, *The Best Years of the "Century": Richard Watson Gilder, "Scribner's Monthly," and the "Century Magazine", 1870–1901*. Urbana: University of Illinois Press, 1981. One of the comprehensive studies of Dodge's circle.

Kaye, Marilyn. Afterword to *Hans Brinker: or The Silver Skates: A Story of Life in Holland*. Signet Classic ed. New York: New American Library, 1986. Contains an analysis of the structure of *Hans Brinker*.

Kelly, R. Gordon. *Children's Periodicals of the United States*. Westport, Conn.: Greenwood Press, 1984.

———. *Mother Was a Lady: Self and Society in Selected American Children's Periodicals, 1865–1890*. Westport, Conn.: Greenwood Press, 1974. A good analysis of the cultural climate that controlled publishing for children.

Lanes, Selma. *Down the Rabbit Hole: Adventures and Misadventures in the Realm of Children's Literature*. New York: Atheneum, 1971. Explores the relationship between *St. Nicholas* and the changes in American society.

Meyers, Annie Nathan. *Barnard Beginnings*. Boston: Houghton Mifflin, 1935. Describes Dodge's support for a college for women, to be connected with Columbia College in New York.

Mott, Frank Luther. *A History of American Magazines*, vol. 3. Cambridge, Mass. Harvard University Press, 1938. An overview of periodical publishing between 1865 and 1885, with chapters on *Scribner's Monthly* and *St. Nicholas*.

Runkle, Lucia Gilbert. "Mary Mapes Dodge." In *Our Famous Women, Comprising the Lives and Deeds of American Women Who Have Distinguished Themselves in Literature. Science, Art, Music, and the Drama, or Are Famous as Heroines, Patriots, Orators, Educators, Physicians, Philanthropists, etc. With Numerous Anecdotes, Incidents and Personal Experiences*. Hartford, Conn: A. D. Worthington, 1884. A personal memoir by a close friend of Dodge's who was also a professional journalist.

Saler, Elizabeth C., and Edwin H. Cady. "The *St. Nicholas* and the Serious Artist." In *Essays Mostly on Periodical Publishing in America: A Collection in Honor of Clarence Gohdes,* edited by James Woodress with the assistance of Townsend Ludington and Joseph Arpad. Durham, N.C.: Duke University Press, 1973. Discusses *St. Nicholas* and its relations to the controversy over literary realism of the time.

Smith, Herbert, *Richard Watson Gilder.* New York: Twayne Publishers, 1975. A concise study of the work of one of Dodge's close colleagues.

Stedman, Edmund C. *Poets of America,* vol. 1. Cambridge, Mass.: Riverside Press, 1885. A survey of American poetry by an influential critic of Dodge's day: touches briefly on her poetry.

Sturges, Florence Stanley. "The *St. Nicholas* Years." In *The Hewins Lectures, 1947–1962,* edited by Siri Andrews. Boston: Horn Book, 1963. An influential but not always accurate account of Dodge's achievements; perpetuates the errors found in Howard.

Tutwiler, Julia. "Mary Mapes Dodge in New York." In *Women Authors of Our Day in Their Homes: Personal Descriptions and Interviews,* edited by Francis Whiting Halsey. New York: James Pott, 1903. Based on an interview with Dodge; describes both her personal and her professional life; important for the story of the naming of *St. Nicholas.*

Twain, Mark. *Letters to His Publishers, 1867–1894,* edited by Hamlin Hill. Berkeley and Los Angeles: University of California Press, 1967. Documents the editorial relationship between Dodge and Twain.

Wheeler, Candace. *Yesterdays in a Busy Life.* New York: Harper & Brothers, 1918. Gives a detailed description of the Onteora artists' community and Dodge's social involvement there.

Wright, Catharine Morris. *Lady of the Silver Skates: The Life and Correspondence of Mary Mapes Dodge.* Jamestown, R. I.: Clingstone Press, 1979. Important biography because it is based on family papers and letters not available elsewhere; does not deal critically with the works.

Journal Articles

Clarke, William Fayal. "In Memory of Mary Mapes Dodge." *St. Nicholas,* October 1905, 1059–1071.

———. "Fifty Years of Saint Nicholas: A Brief Anniversary Compilation of Chronicle and Comment." *St. Nicholas,* November 1923, 16–23.

"Culture and Progress." *Scribner's Monthly,* November 1876, 36.

Erisman, Fred R. "The Utopia of *St. Nicholas*: The Present as Prologue." *Children's Literature* 5 (1976): 66–73.

Gilder, Jeannette. "The Newark Life of Mary Mapes Dodge." *Critic* 47, no. 4 (October 1905): 292.

Griswold, Jerome. *"Hans Brinker*: Sunny World, Angry Waters." *Children's Literature* 12 (1984): 47–60.

"The Little Dutch Hero." *Boy's Own Magazine*, 1855, 292–93.

"The Little Dykeman." Translated from the French of Madame Eugénie Foa. *Old Merry's Annual* (1871): 638–40.

McEnery, Sarah S. "Mary Mapes Dodge: An Intimate Tribute." *Critic* 47, no. 4 (October 1905): 310–12.

"Recent Fiction." *Century*, August 1885, 657.

Sircar, Sanjay. "The Victorian Auntly Voice and Mrs. Molesworth's *Cuckoo Clock*." *Children's Literature* 17 (1989): 1–24.

Stern, Madeleine. "Louisa Alcott's Self-Criticism." In *Studies in the American Renaissance*, edited by Joel Myerson. Charlottesville: University Press of Virginia, 1988.

Wright, Catharine Morris. "How *St. Nicholas* Got Rudyard Kipling: And What Happened Then." *Princeton University Library Chronicle* 35 (Spring 1974): 259–89.

Scholarly Papers

Erisman, Fred R. "There Was a Child Went Forth: A Study of *St. Nicholas Magazine* and Selected Children's Authors, 1890–1915." Ph.D. diss., University of Minnesota, 1966.

Fuller, Lawrence B. "Mary Mapes Dodge and *St. Nicholas:* The Development of a Philosophy and Practice of Publishing for Young People." Paper presented at the annual meeting of the National Council of Teachers of English, Detroit, Michigan, November 1984: ERIC Educational Document, ED 251 847.

Rahn, Suzanne, "*St. Nicholas* and Its Friends: The Magazine-Child Relationship 100 Years Ago." Paper presented at the annual meeting of the Research Society for Victorian Periodicals, San Marino, California, September 1989.

Roggenbuck, Mary June. "*St. Nicholas Magazine*: A Study of the Impact and Historical Influence of the Editorship of Mary Mapes Dodge." Ph.D. diss., University of Michigan, 1976.

Index

The Authors

Susan R. Gannon received her A.B. from the College of New Rochelle and her Ph.D. from Fordham University. She is professor of literature and communications at Pace University, where she teaches eighteenth- and nineteenth-century literature and children's literature. She is book review editor of the *Children's Literature Association Quarterly* and from 1985 to 1990 coedited the *Proceedings* of the Children's Literature Association's annual conferences. She has published on Stevenson, on Collodi, and on critical approaches to children's literature.

Ruth Anne Thompson received her A.B. from the College of New Rochelle and her Ph.D. from Fordham University. She is associate professor of literature and communications at Pace University, where she teaches writing and literature and serves as associate dean of Dyson College. From 1985 to 1990 she coedited the *Proceedings* of the Children's Literature Association's annual conferences. Her primary interests are in the nineteenth-century novel and in periodical publishing for children.

The Editor

Ruth K. MacDonald is professor of English and head of the Department of English and Philosophy at Purdue University Calumet, Hammond, Indiana. She has contributed the volumes on Louisa May Alcott, Beatrix Potter, and Dr. Seuss to Twayne's United States and English Authors Series and has written two other books on children's literature. She earned her B.A. and M.A. in English from the University of Connecticut, her Ph.D. in English from Rutgers—The State University of New Jersey, and her M.B.A. from the University of Texas at El Paso.